Writing Guidelines
for Science and Applied Science Students

Writing Guidelines
for Science and
Applied Science Students

Lisa Emerson and John Hampton (Eds)

CENGAGE
Learning™

Australia • Brazil • Japan • Korea • Mexico • Singapore • Spain • United Kingdom • United States

CENGAGE
Learning·

Writing Guidelines for Science and Applied Science Students
1st Edition
Edited by Lisa Emerson and John Hampton

Publishing editor: Sharmian Firth
Project editor: Chris Wyness
Cover design: Olga Lavecchia
Production crontroller: Carly Imrie
Reprint: Magda Koralewska

Any URLs contained in this publication were checked for currency during the production process. Note, however, that the publisher cannot vouch for the ongoing currency of URLs.

First published as *Writing Guidelines for Business Students* by Dunmore Press in 1995.

Printed in Australia by Ligare Pty Limited.
8 9 10 11 12 13 14 19 18 17 16 15

For product information and technology assistance,
in Australia call **1300 790 853**;
in New Zealand call **0800 449 725**

For permission to use material from this text or product, please email
aust.permissions@cengage.com

ISBN 978 0 17 021494 0

Cengage Learning Australia
Level 7, 80 Dorcas Street
South Melbourne, Victoria Australia 3205

Cengage Learning New Zealand
Unit 4B Rosedale Office Park
331 Rosedale Road, Albany, North Shore 0632, NZ

For learning solutions, visit **cengage.com.au**

Contents

Preface

As students in a science or applied science course, you are involved in scientific writing. The purpose of scientific writing is to communicate scientific findings in a way that can be received and understood by the intended audience. Scientific writing should therefore be as clear and as simple as possible.

> Clear communication, which is the prime objective of scientific writing, may be achieved by presenting ideas in an orderly manner and by expressing oneself smoothly and precisely. By developing ideas clearly and logically, you invite readers to read, encourage them to continue, and make their task agreeable by leading them smoothly from thought to thought.
>
> *Publication Manual of the American Psychological Association*

There are many kinds of writing. At school or in later education, at some stage you took English and were encouraged to write creatively. Your work dealt with emotions and opinions, and your marks were better if you used language devices such as similes, metaphors and other figures of speech. However, as Day (1992, p. 1) puts it, 'there is a world of difference between creative writing and scientific writing'. Scientific writing:

- is the factual recording of the results of scientific investigation
- is as clear and as simple as possible
- requires polished writing skills.

In scientific writing, if you use excessive verbiage and flowery language you will more than likely lose the reader and fail to communicate your scientific findings. Is this important? Definitely! Science is based on the fundamental assumption that original research must be published, because only in this way can new scientific findings be authenticated and added to the existing database we call scientific knowledge. A scientific experiment, no matter how spectacular the results, is not completed until the results are published. Scientists must therefore not only carry out research, they must write!

As you already know, modern science contends with complex and complicated problems and the language scientists use 'must be capable of precise descriptions of complex problems and concepts' (Day, 1992). English has become the universal language of science. If you take up a career in science or applied science, you may find yourself attending a scientific conference in Beijing or Brussels or submitting a scientific paper to an international journal edited in Paris or Perugia. In each case, the language used will be English.

For science writing, directness and clarity are the key issues:

> ... *the best English is that which gives the sense in the fewest short words.*
>
> *Journal of Bacteriology,* Instructions to Authors

This is what you should be aiming for in your writing.

1. Introduction

The purpose of this manual is to introduce writers studying science or applied science to the standard requirements for assignments. It looks at the structures of research reports, business reports and essays and recommends methods of presenting data and formatting sources. The Appendices outline elements of style – how to write more clearly, how to avoid clumsy terms and sexist language. The Reference Section provides a list of resources you might find useful if you feel you need more detailed assistance in a particular aspect of writing.

Written assignments are an unavoidable aspect of a student's life; they serve several purposes. First, they are, of course, a method of assessing and evaluating student performance – but that is not all. The process of finding, analysing, organising and presenting information is an invaluable aid to learning. This process of writing an assignment, painful as it may seem at times, helps you understand and integrate new information and material. Finally, learning to convey information on paper in a clear and professional manner is part of student training for a career in applied science. Whether you plan a life on a farm, in a lab, as a consultant or in an industry-related field, there will be times when you will need to be able to communicate effectively. Employer surveys conducted by Australian and New Zealand universities constantly highlight the need for graduates with a high standard of communication skills – spoken and written. Learning to write professionally is, then, part of the **content** of the curriculum, of your study programme – it is a measure of your credibility.

This Manual is intended as a guide. If any of your assignment requirements do not appear to fit the formats described here you should always consult your course coordinator, lecturer or tutor. Be flexible in your approach and be prepared to adapt your format to suit the specific requirements of different papers and teachers.

1.1   Assignment Presentation

Procedures for presenting assignments are detailed in this section. Individual courses may have different procedures; always check the course outline or assignment directions for your specific papers.

Professional Appearance

Students often underestimate the value of presenting their work well; this is a mistake. The visual impact of your assignment **does** influence your marker(s). You are undergoing professional training; for this reason, the person marking your work will expect you to produce work which would appear credible in the work environment. You do not want your writing to convey the impression that you are a careless person.

Do not fill the entire page, solidly, with print. Set off the print with lots of white space; your assignment will be easier to read, and important points will stand out.

Print on one side of the page only.

Headings, sub-headings, tables, diagrams and graphs can improve the appearance of a written project. It is important to be consistent in the use of aids within a report (see Section 9 and Appendix A on presentation of data and headings).

All assignments should have a title page.

1.2   Margin for Marker's Comments

Leave a 3 cm space along the left-hand margin of each page of your assignment. You will get more useful feedback if markers have room to respond as they are reading. The text should be 1.5 or 2.0 spaced to provide additional room for editorial comments.

1.3   Typing your Assignment

Most courses already specify (in course outlines) that assignments be typed. Even if typing is not required, it is advisable. Word processing means you can more easily edit your document and present it professionally. If you do not have your own computer most tertiary institutions have computer facilities available.

1.4   Responsibility for Taking a Copy

There is always a risk of an assignment being lost. Make a copy of your work before handing one in for marking. Burn your assignment onto a CD or copy to disk. Without a copy, if your assignment should be misplaced, you will have to rewrite the assignment or forfeit the marks: the responsibility to make a copy is **yours**.

1.5   Correct Use of English

Like the visual appearance of your work, the correctness of your grammar, word-usage, punctuation and spelling will influence the marker. In some papers a percentage of the mark is given to language use. For tertiary level work you are expected to understand and apply the basic rules of English.

Most libraries keep reference books on English rules and style (some of which are listed in the Reference and Bibliography section on pp. 93 and 94). If you think you have writing difficulties which require help, you should check out student learning services on your campus.

Even if you have good English skills, take the time to proofread your work. Spelling and other types of careless mistakes distract the marker and diminish their sense of your professionalism. You should own a good dictionary – and use it often. Con't rely on the spellchecker on your computer - it will not pick up all errors.

1.6   Plagiarism

Copying another person's ideas or words without acknowledgement is called plagiarism. This includes copying material from the Internet or other electronice sources. It is a grave academic and legal offence. It is viewed very seriously by academic staff and the penalties can be severe. Discuss your assignments with fellow students, by all means, but the work you submit for marking must be your own work. If you want to quote someone else's work in your assignment, the author and original source of this work must be clearly shown. It is important that you understand how to use secondary sources correctly so read Chapters 11 and 12 carefully.

1.7   References

For many assignments you will need to consult articles, books and other published materials. The list of references used in compiling your work should be attached to the assignment (see Section 12, p. 99 for details on how this list should be formatted).

1.8   Handing in Assignments

Most courses specify due dates for assignments. Buy yourself a wall planner and as soon as you are provided with these due dates, plot them on the wall planner. Make sure you write the dates of all assignments for all your courses on the wall planner. You can then plan for particularly demanding periods, such as the end of term dates, when many assignments are due. Try not to fall behind with your assignments. Some course coordinators do not accept late assignments; others take off a percentage of the mark for work submitted late. But even if no penalty exists for late assignments, you need to pace your work so that you do not get out of step with other assignments.

2. Information Skills for Science and Technology

You have a vast amount of information available to you from the media, the internet, from lecturers and friends and from the books and journals held in your library. When you are looking for information for your assignments the material you find must pass a number of tests. It must be

- Relevant
- Understandable
- True

Keep these factors in mind when considering the usefulness of a particular source.

2.1 An Information Strategy

Before you begin looking for information on your topic, set out a broad plan of how you will proceed. Your strategy will ensure that you have understood your topic and that the information you find is a good match for the subject. Your strategy needs to begin with a clear definition of the topic, including all of the words used.

Let's say you are studying sports science and the topic for your assignment is *"The effect of carbohydrates on endurance in sports and exercise"*. You need to ask yourself the following questions:

- Do I understand what all of these words mean? How could I rephrase the question using other words?
- Can I break the question into parts? What are the major concepts?
- What level of detail do I need? Will a general discussion be sufficient or do I need some detailed examples with statistics?
- Do I need to include very recent sources?

Begin with some background reading to give yourself a broad understanding of the subject. Useful sources would be specialist encyclopedias and dictionaries that will define terms and major concepts. They should also alert you to the existence of differing viewpoints where there is debate about a topic. Note down any relevant words or phrases that are used. An encyclopedia article may well refer you to other more detailed sources of information.

Once you have done this, check your library's catalogue for books on the subject. Be aware that you possibly won't get an entire book devoted to your exact topic, so you might want to search for titles on related subjects. Remember, too, that a single book on the subject will only give the views of its author(s) and you should probably supplement the information from other sources. The references at the end of the book are valuable guides to more information.

If you need more detailed or recent information, start searching for journal articles or conference papers. By this stage you will have a clearer idea of what you are looking for. Journal articles are generally highly specialized reports of research and you can narrow your search down to look for very specific information.

As you locate information, note down the sources you have found, including publication details, page numbers of important passages and so on. This will allow you to accurately reference material when you come to write up your assignment.

Once you have gathered the information (and read at least some of it) you can decide what is likely to be most useful in writing your assignment. Discard anything you may have picked up that is not relevant to the topic of your assignment. Anything that appears to be aimed at a general audience needs to be treated with caution unless it is quoting actual research. Look at the remaining information you have found. Do the views presented in some of the books or articles contradict those found in others? If more recent work differs markedly from older research you are probably looking at a field that is changing over time and you should make sure you have a good representation of recent material. Some areas of research are marked by ongoing differences of opinion between various experts and you may need to take more than one approach into account, even those you disagree with.

2.2   Sources of Information

Encyclopedias and Dictionaries

Many of the information sources available contain specialised information and require some existing level of knowledge. Before you embark on searching for books or articles, consult specialist encyclopedias, dictionaries and handbooks to give yourself a basic knowledge of the field and access to a body of factual information. Some encyclopedias will have articles written and signed by specialists who can be relied upon to give an authoritative account of their subjects.

Advantages of reference books:

- ❏ You can save time by ensuring that you understand the terms and concepts
- ❏ You can learn "a little about a lot" and acquire a broader understanding of your subject
- ❏ You can quickly find out who the classic authors in a field are and get some view of its history
- ❏ You have a good source of facts
- ❏ Many online encyclopedias are regularly updated

Disadvantages

- ❏ Reference books can be quite dated – even at the time of publication they are probably not cutting edge
- ❏ It can be difficult to find the right reference book for your topic
- ❏ With some general titles the coverage can be quite superficial.

Books

In many circumstances a book will be the most useful source of information on your topic. Its extended treatment can give you essential background information and plenty of explanation and it is often possible to find a book aimed at your level of knowledge of the topic. Most introductory texts will be written by one or more authors, whereas for a more advanced treatment of the topic you can find an edited book where each chapter is written by an expert on that particular aspect of the subject.

Books:

- ❏ Can give you everything you need to know about the topic from one source
- ❏ Are a good starting point that will give you an overview of your topic
- ❏ Using the index you can find quite specific information
- ❏ You can read them on the bus, or wherever.

But:

- ❏ They tend not to be "cutting edge" as they take quite a time to write and publish
- ❏ Often it's more difficult to track down very specific information in books because they are not indexed electronically
- ❏ Only one person can read them at a time and the one you want is always out!

You find books by using your library's catalogue which lists the author, title and publishing details of each book and also subject keywords and even chapter headings. Most libraries hold classes for students on how to use their catalogue, and library staff will be keen to help you master the art of finding books.

Journal Articles

In the academic and research world, journals are important. In format they are very similar to the magazines, but in importance and value they are at the top of the heap. Most scientific research is reported in the form of journal articles that describe the purpose of the study, the methods used, the results found and the conclusions drawn. These articles are written by experts for a specialised audience and will assume that their readers are already familiar with the topic. Most journal articles tend to be about a very specific subject rather than giving a general treatment of a wide area of knowledge.

Reputable academic journals require the articles they publish to undergo a quality control process known as "peer reviewing". An article sent to the journal to be published will first be sent to one or more people who are expert in the area that the article is about. They may reject the article outright or require changes to be made before it is able to be published. By referring to peer-reviewed (or "refereed") articles, you help ensure that what you write is based on scrutinised material.

Most journals are published in a "volume and issue" format. *The Journal of Robotic Systems* is a monthly journal, meaning that a new issue comes out each month. Twelve issues of the journal make up a volume which will have its own number and then each issue has a number as well. As well as monthly issues, bimonthly (every two months) and quarterly (every three months) formats are quite common.

You normally locate journal articles by searching databases (see below). Many researchers browse one or two of their favourite journals every month, but when you want to find specific information browsing is not effective. Many journals nowadays put their contents on the Internet but you need to be aware that the actual articles themselves are usually not freely available to the public.

When you have identified an article you want to read, search the library catalogue by Journal title to see whether your library owns it. You may even have to check whether the exact issue is held. The catalogue will tell you only whether the Library holds the journal; it contains no information about the articles. It is increasingly common for journals to be available electronically rather than in print, but even if you have accessed it electronically, you still deal with it as if it were a print copy, quoting volumes and issues, page numbers and so on. Regardless of whether the journal is electronic or print, your library catalogue should be the definitive list of what is available to you.

It is not necessary to confine your research to academic peer-reviewed journals. Sometimes "trade journals" are valuable and more "popular-level" titles can be useful for news and comment. Journals are also referred to as "periodicals" and "serials".

Journal articles usually begin with an abstract, a summary of their contents. This is useful in helping you decide whether to read the whole article and also comes in very handy when we are searching for articles on databases.

Journal articles are:
- Written and checked by experts
- Very up-to-date in their coverage and include information that hasn't yet made it into books
- Provide very detailed information
- Written on a huge range of topics

Disadvantages are
- If the subject is a technical one you probably need to know quite a bit about it before you can read journal articles
- It can be hard to get an overview of the topic - articles can be quite narrow in their scope
- You can be overwhelmed by the sheer volume of information.

Conferences

Researchers often present their findings as a conference paper, a written version of the conference presentation. These can be even more up-to-the-minute than articles. Some time after the conference, the papers presented will be published in a volume called the "Proceedings" of the conference.

Conference papers can be harder to find than books and articles and they are not included in many databases. Even when you have a reference to a conference paper it can be difficult to locate on the library catalogue. As with book chapters, you can't look up the name of the author or the paper but you must search for the name of the conference. Locating conference proceedings can be difficult, so check with library staff on how to do this.

Databases

Like the library catalogue, electronic databases are made up of records but in this case they are descriptions of journal articles and sometimes book chapters and conference papers, and sometimes the articles themselves in electronic format.

Usually we access these databases over the internet, but as they are not publicly available (access is paid for by your institution and is for students and staff only) you do not generally refer to them as you would to information found on a website. Nor do you generally refer to a database as if it were an information source even when you find a full-text article. The original source of the article is still the journal and you generally cite it as if you had seen the print version, including volume, issue and page numbers.

This is not the place to describe the full complexities of database searching. If your library holds classes on database searching, you should attend them or ask a library staff member to give you advice, any handouts they have and maybe a lesson.

2.3   Other Sources of Information

While science and technology stress formal publication channels to report on research, a wealth of information is available on the internet and in the popular media. If you are interested in social or political aspects of your subject, newspapers may give better coverage than scientific journals, and the internet will give you access to a huge range of opinion and relevant organizations.

The Internet

The Internet is an information tool used daily by millions of researchers, students and librarians to find information that might otherwise have taken them days to find by traditional means. You can use it as an encyclopedia, a dictionary, a newspaper and a conference. Learn to use a good Search Engine and don't waste time following irrelevant links!!

Electronic database search techniques allow you to:

❑ Search the contents of journals at the one time
❑ Find matches to your search terms anywhere in the references to articles, even if the word you are looking for is in the middle of the title or halfway through a 300 word abstract
❑ Look for matches using a complex set of terms
❑ Use *word truncation* techniques to cover different endings of a word and *wildcards* for spelling variants
❑ Ask for references where two words are close to but not next to one another – "*coffee* consumption by *students* ". This is known as Proximity searching.

Electronic information sources vary quite a lot but they generally:

❑ Search records that are a "cut-down" version of the full document (though you can sometimes search the full document as well)
❑ Use the same "logic" in the way they put terms together.

The Media (Newspapers, TV and Radio)

Much useful information comes to us through television and radio news, newspaper and magazine stories, and articles. Many newspapers have their latest editions on the web but you may need to go to a database to get full coverage of previous editions.

Media information has these advantages:

- ❑ It is usually very up-to-date and international
- ❑ It is easy to understand and often includes explanation, comment and analysis
- ❑ It will tend to show more than one side of the issue and summarise different points of view
- ❑ It may include expert comment
- ❑ It may place scientific and technological issues in their social and political context
- ❑ In some areas it is the best or only source of information.

And these disadvantages:

- ❑ Much of the information consists of untested comments and assertions which can be difficult to sort out from proven facts and tested theories
- ❑ It may oversimplify and sensationalise issues – in science and technology the media tend to present stories as either "breakthroughs" or "scares"
- ❑ Media information, especially items from radio and television, can be hard to trace after a relatively short period of time.

2.4   Storing and Using Information

As you work on your assignment you may need to find more information and follow new leads that arise from what you have read.

Many students and researchers use specialist software like EndNote, ProCite or Reference Manager to store their references and to output them in the appropriate bibliographic style. If you struggle with recording information, or if are undertaking a major project, it would be a good idea to check with your library to see if you can purchase a copy.

Good information searching and management will improve the quality of your work and save time. Thorough searching and careful documenting of sources should mean that you don't have to keep covering the same ground or hunting for lost references. Scientists and technologists are heavy consumers of knowledge. The information skills you learn as a student will continue to be used throughout your career.

3. Notetaking

Generally students take notes when they attend lectures or field trips and when they are reading study material such as books or articles. There is no one correct approach to taking notes and individual students use different techniques depending on their personal learning styles, habits and experience. Different students also focus on different aspects during a lecture and hence take notes which emphasise these different aspects. Taking notes is highly personal and what is described here will give you a few useful suggestions which you can adapt and modify to your own personal situation.

3.1   Why Take Notes?

There are several reasons for taking notes, which include:

- Preparing and revising for exams.
- Researching for assignments.
- Expanding knowledge in a field.
- Helping you to remember material.
- Organising thought processes.
- Achieving deep processing of information.

Perhaps the first four reasons mentioned above are the most commonly given reasons for taking notes. But what most people do not know is that if notes are carefully and systematically taken they enhance your ability to understand a subject at a much deeper and more complex level. And this is, after all, the aim of true learning.

3.2   The Relationship between Notetaking and Memory

Most students seem to know instinctively that taking notes helps memory. We will consider very briefly how memory works in relation to notetaking.

The key to improving memory is to interact with new material and to repeat it. We remember things that are interesting or meaningful to us. Also, memory is located in the synaptic connection that occurs in the brain – very much like a charge of electricity. The more times this electrical connection is made, the stronger the connection becomes, hence the stronger the memory becomes.

This is why reviewing notes is so important. It has been shown that if information is reviewed within 24 hours of first learning the chances of remembering it are increased by up to 60 per cent. A suggested review plan is:

- Review within 24 hours.
- Review after one week.
- Review after one month.
- Review again in six months.

But it is the notes that should be reviewed and not the original material. The notes that you have made serve as a trace of your interaction with the material and enable you to remember. Notes remind you of your original responses to the material.

Another important principle concerning memory and notetaking is visualisation. Human beings have phenomenal visual memories. Consider how many people's faces you have stored in your memory. You may not remember names but you can instantly recognise a face you have not seen for years among a crowd of strangers. Turning new material into something visual is a very powerful way of aiding learning, memory and understanding. And one way of doing this is by creating a mind map (covered later in this chapter) with new information. Writing notes in the margin of a textbook also works in a similar way by aiding visualisation.

3.3   What is the Benefit of Taking Notes?

One of the most valuable things about taking notes is that it forces you to articulate the ideas that you are hearing/reading. In putting ideas into your own words, you begin to understand them. After understanding comes memory. It is much easier to remember something which has meaning for you and which you understand. Therefore, when working through study material, you should be making notes to begin the process of understanding, which will lead later to deep processing and better memory of the material.

Interaction with material is another way of helping your brain to remember because you make mental connections all the time. Do this by making notes in the margins of your study guides as well.

3.4   Steps to Follow While Taking Notes

As mentioned above, different techniques of notetaking are appropriate for different purposes. Sometimes the most useful thing to do is to get an overview of a piece of writing. This is especially good if you are planning to take notes on an entire book. Even with short articles gaining an overview can sometimes be of tremendous use.

The following steps can be used for taking good notes:

1. Wait

- Sometimes it can be very useful to gain an overview of a reading or book before taking notes. There are various ways to do this and some examples are described below.
- Before taking notes you should have in mind the purpose of the notes. Are you taking notes at a lecture, at a field lab, or from a textbook? Are the notes for an exam or for research? The answers to these questions will affect the method you use and the amount of detail needed in your notes. One of the most important principles of good notetaking is flexibility; you should be able to take sketchy notes at times and detailed notes at other times and to judge which approach is more appropriate.
- Never start writing immediately. Whether you are reading study material or listening to a farmer, you should first try to understand what is being said, and then try to simplify it in your own words. The aim of taking notes is to arrive at understanding first and then make the information memorable/meaningful for your own brain.

Try to focus on key words or ideas. This is easier said than done. For example, sometimes learning about a new subject, which has lots of new jargon, can be overwhelming. Trying to extract the key words and ideas can seem an impossible task. The best advice in this situation is to persevere. As you become more familiar with the subject area and begin to feel less overwhelmed by so many new and unfamiliar terms, key words and ideas will become apparent. Unfortunately, most students experience a steep learning curve before they understand new concepts well.

2. Identify

- In lectures take down the name of the lecturer, the course details and the date. This will make it easier to manage your notes (and file them) later. Also, using the same size paper makes organising your notes easier.
- While taking notes for an assignment, it is important to record where the information came from. You may want, at a later stage, to refer back to the original material for clarification or you may wish to cite or quote the material in your assignment. At the top of the page write down the date and publication

information. Make a note of the title, author, publisher and date of publication (see page 86 for more information on referencing).

3. Space

- Allow plenty of space in your notes so that when you revise, additional notes can be made. Three methods of notetaking are described on page 24 – the Linear, Princeton and Mind Mapping systems. Even if you have developed a preferred system of notetaking, it is sometimes useful to try different approaches.
- Your writing should not be too small because it will be hard to read later. If you are creating mind maps, consider using A3 paper which will allow plenty of space for pictures and diagrams.

4. Key Points

- Having a broad knowledge of what the article or book contains at the outset, will allow you to better isolate key points.
- Except for quotations (which must be taken down in full and absolutely accurately), you should not take down word for word what you read or hear. Many students make the mistake of overwriting; they write down too much.
- In a lecture situation listen carefully to what is being said and then summarise briefly what you understand. If a lecture has been properly constructed this is not too difficult as lecturers tend to repeat important points or write them on a board.
- When reading study material always try to understand a point first and then select **key words** to write down. Depending on the length of a paragraph, it is better to first grasp the meaning before taking anything down. As a rough guide, try to comprehend a few paragraphs (or a page of text) before making any notes.

5. Interact

Your own notes are the best place to help you develop your opinions about what you are reading or hearing. When writing assignments you are often expected to express a personal opinion or evaluation. These ideas are formed during the reading and notetaking you undertake before writing the assignment. As you take notes you can make observations and note comparisons, interesting points, authorial attitudes, points of cross-reference or contradiction. The point of doing this is because you want your mind to engage with the ideas – which helps comprehension and memory.

Once you have taken your notes and organised them, you can develop trigger words or mnemonics to help you remember key points. If a text belongs to you, write summaries and key words in the margins, perhaps even questions.

The more interaction you can incorporate into your learning, the more efficiently you will be able to learn. Remember, reviewing notes (another way of interacting) soon after first learning is one of the best ways to facilitate understanding and memory.

3.5   Gaining an Overview of Study Material

As suggested earlier, having an overview can help you to process information, understand it, and remember it. When making notes on an entire book or an article, an overview can be gained by scanning the material first so that you know what it contains.

If you are reading a book, examine the contents page, index, date of publication, and any diagrams. The date of publication is important because it tells you if the book and its ideas are current. Scanning the introduction is also a good way to get a quick sense of what is covered in the book. You will be able to approach the reading and notetaking with a superficial understanding of what is contained in the article. In effect you will have a framework of ideas in your mind onto which you can later pin key ideas. You can do much the same kind of overview for articles, by quickly scanning headings and subheadings.

A very economical way to take notes without reading every word is to only read the topic sentence of each paragraph. Usually the topic sentence contains a summary of the rest of the paragraph and it usually comes near the beginning of the paragraph. At most you will be reading the first one or two sentences of a paragraph. This method is very useful because you can use it to quickly check whether an article is useful to refresh your memory on something already read, or gain a quick (yet surprisingly detailed) overview of an article before reading it in more depth. This is a skill worth acquiring!

3.6   Taking Notes on a Field Trip

Some courses – such as those in agriculture or horticulture – require notetaking on field trips. Taking notes on a field trip requires you to be organised: there is only one chance to acquire all the information you need.

Be prepared. Make sure you understand the **purpose** of the trip. Are you expected to write a report based on the field trip and, if so, what information is needed to complete the report? Design a series of questions to ensure that you get all the information you need from the farmer or grower. Sometimes it is useful to organise a group who can work through the questions. You might designate different jobs for different members of your group, e.g. someone to ask questions, someone to write down answers, someone to observe in particular areas.

Once you are on site, listen carefully to the grower/farmer, and to the questions asked by other students or accompanying staff members. Make sure you have answers to all of your own questions and take notes on any questions you had not considered. A tape-recorder might be used to tape discussions but always have pen and paper with you for back-up in case you find yourself in a noisy environment where voices will not be picked up on a tape.

After the trip, revisit your notes as soon as possible. Fill in any gaps in your

notes and make sure you can read everything you have written down (notes written in the field are notoriously illegible!). Rewrite, or write a summary containing all the key ideas. If you have used a tape, summarise the tape.

3.7 Different Approaches to Taking Notes

The three different methods of notetaking that we will examine are: the Linear (or logical outline) System, the Princeton Method and Mind Mapping.

1. The *Linear System* is probably the most commonly used of all notetaking methods and is the best for certain types of information, e.g. detailed facts. A

common error is that people take down too much information, rather than simple key words.

To use this method, subdivide your notes into paragraphs and sections using indentations of varying depth. Indicate the subdivisions with headings, numbers and other symbols.

The limitation with this method is that it may be difficult to organise or connect concepts in the notes, depending on the complexity of the subjects. Perhaps you might like to take notes like this and then later organise the ideas into a mind map.

For example: Study Skills

1. Notetaking
   1.1   Linear System
         (i)
         (ii)
   1.2   Princeton Method
         (i)
         (ii)
   1.3   Mind Mapping

2. The *Princeton Method* is very simple and gives you space for rereading and responding to notes.

   Divide your page into three columns. The first column is used for the heading and main points and the second for the summary. The third column is really useful for reviewing your notes. Or you can note things you did not recall, examples, your own personal comments or a summary of the middle column.

3. *Mind Maps*. If you know how to use this method you will find it has unexpected advantages. First, you have to organise your thoughts as you draw the concept-tree, which is an excellent aid to memory. Second, mind maps are visual and the chance of you being able to remember the visual elements (and the information) is greatly enhanced.

Headings, main points, etc.	Summary of the notes	Blank column to use for ideas that come into your head when reading, for examples or for making a briefer summary at exam time.

Making mind maps is a great aid to learning but it does require additional investment of time. Even if you do not want to take your initial notes using this method, there are several other ways to use it. You can use mind maps to plan tasks, read and research, plan and write assignments, and to revise and plan for exams.

When you are drawing a mind map:

- Select a brief phrase (one or two words) and/or picture which describes the topic, e.g. Study Skills.
- Write this phrase or picture in the centre of a blank page.
- Draw branches out from the topic which represent main ideas. Write these main ideas down at the end of the branch. Use only one or two key words, not whole sentences.
- Add further branches to these main ideas to break the idea down into finer detail.
- Indicate associations between separate branches by connecting lines.
- Use as much colour and as many symbols or pictures as possible.
- Allow plenty of space. Use A3 sheets of paper for very complex mind maps.

The notetaking method you use will depend on you and the subject area, but this skill is invaluable for tertiary study.

3.8   A Word of Caution

When taking notes, always indicate in your notes if you copy from another source directly. If you fail to do this, you may then forget this is a quote and copy it into your assignment and then, inadvertently, plagiarise. Always put quotation marks around a quotation in your notes and include source details and a page number for future reference.

4. The Writing Process

Inexperienced writers tend to assume that writing has two stages: the first draft and the final copy. In fact, writing should be a **process** that contains many stages. Students should organise their time wisely to allow sufficient time to do justice to each stage. Everyone has their own approach to the writing process; this chapter outlines various stages students may go through while writing an assignment.

4.1   What Does the Marker Want?

Look carefully at the assignment topic and any directions given by the lecturer. Most lecturers design assignment questions for a specific purpose. Ask yourself the following questions:

- What format should I use?
    - report
    - essay
    - review
    - other

- Who is my audience?
    - lecturer
    - peer
    - client

- Do I understand the subject?
    - broad issues
    - narrowing.

Make sure you are fully aware of what is required **before** starting to gather or analyse information; you may waste a lot of time if you do not attend to this first step.

4.2   Generate Your Own Ideas

Ask yourself "What can I say that is relevant now?" Try:

- Brainstorming or free writing – writing down any words, phrases or ideas that come to you (no matter how irrelevant or silly they may appear), eliminating those which are not appropriate, and selecting those with which you can do more serious, focused thinking.
- Clustering – connecting and linking the ideas, and then linking them back to your subject/topic.
- Asking questions about the topic (hint: use the Wh-questions; Who? What? When? Where? Why?).

Have confidence in your own ideas, thoughts and intelligence!

4.3   Gathering Information

The nature and amount of information needed will depend on the requirements of the particular assignment.

e.g.   industry visit/field trip assignment = the notes you took during your visit plus relevant background information and data.

research report = published scientific papers, reviews and reports.

For more detail on how to acquire information see Chapter 2, p. 12.

You will at some stage need to use published material (book, scientific paper, review, popular article, newspaper). Get into the habit of collecting your material systematically – this will save time in the long run. Take the following steps:

- Write down the basic bibliographical information (use a card system, not scraps of paper which get lost!). For a scientific paper write down the author(s), publication date, title, journal name, volume number, page numbers, e.g. Brown, D.B. 1996: Effluent disposal from dairy farms. *Journal of environment and agriculture 64:* 271–276. For books include the publisher and place of publication (see Chapter 12, p. 99).
- Alternatively, learn to use a referencing database system such as Procite or Endnote. Many tertiary institutions run short courses on how to use these very efficient time-saving systems.
- If you decide to quote from the text, be exact. Use quotation marks to indicate

it is a direct quotation. Make a note of the page numbers so that you can cite them in the text (see Chapter 12, p. 100), and also so that you can find the passage again.

- Do not collect information/data mindlessly. Read critically, keeping the particular assignment task in mind and making sure the material is relevant.

4.4 Focusing

Generating techniques such as brainstorming, clustering and questioning, plus your reading of the literature may present you with the problem of **too much information** or **too many possibilities**. Focus on what is potentially significant by asking yourself:

- Is my topic narrow enough?
- Will it sustain interest?
- Is it appropriate to my intended audience?
- Are there enough aspects for development to the required length?
- Do I have enough supporting material to work with?

Always ask yourself "what is the key question my assignment should answer?".

4.5 Drafting

Drafting – writing the first draft of an assignment – is perhaps the most difficult, frustrating – and, surprisingly at times, exhilarating – part of the writing process.

Allow plenty of time for drafting. You are unlikely to write anything perfectly at first try. You must write and rewrite. If you have a word processor the process may be a little easier. Generally, the more drafts you do, the better the final version.

So, you have a pile of notes, statistics and printouts beside you and a clutter of ideas in your head. How do you organise it all? Karen Rhodes (English Department 2003) identifies the following steps:

- Find a favourite location in a comfortable (and **quiet**) place. Get together all your supplies. Make yourself inaccessible: the library, which is full of acquaintances and friends who may lure you into the coffee bar, is not a good place for drafting.
- Slowly reread all your notes and carefully review any outline made to guide your work.
- Put all your preliminary notes to one side and write a draft as quickly as

possible. Don't stop. If you are writing an assignment which is structured in sections (e.g. a business report or research report), start with the easiest sections. Don't reread your writing. Skip lines if you have blanks.

- Don't worry about small mistakes, spelling or style and don't linger over small problems. Concentrate on developing your ideas and working out your structure.

Every writer experiences "blocking" at some stage; some of us get mental blocks with alarming regularity! If you do 'get stuck', try to break the block by just writing anything that comes into your head, and then gradually ease yourself into writing about the topic. Another approach is to write down the reasons why you cannot get started (if the problem is defined, you may be able to dispose of it!).

4.6 Revising

Revising can be a deeply satisfying experience.

When you have finished your first draft you should always take a break so that you can come back to your manuscript and see it through fresh, and more detached, eyes. Revision literally means to "re-see". In the revision stage you should focus on the content and structure of your work – again, do not worry about stylistic issues: look at the wood, not the trees.

Ask yourself the following questions:

- Have I done exactly what was required, i.e. does the content match the assignment requirements?
- Do my key ideas stand out clearly?
- Have I supported my key ideas sufficiently, i.e. have I provided enough evidence to convince my reader?
- Does the structure of my work highlight my key ideas? Are they interrelated? Do they form a logical sequence of information?
- Would a different structure aid my reader's understanding?

Adopt the role of the reader; try to see your work through the eyes of someone else. Read through your draft, jotting down in the margin the gist of the subject matter in each of the main sections. This will help you to get a feel for the movement of your ideas and the logic of the structure you have used. Reading your work out aloud (or getting someone to read it to you) may help even more.

4.7   Editing

Editing refers to making changes to sentence structure and replacing words. Your focus should be on readability and style: now is the time to look at the trees rather than the wood.

A direct, vigorous writing style is more likely to catch and hold the attention of busy people. Make each sentence clear and to the point, conveying its information in as few words as possible. Check the following:

• Paragraphs	-	Does each paragraph have a topic sentence?
	-	Does each paragraph have a single subject? (see Appendix C, p. 115.)
	-	Are the paragraphs a reasonable length?
• Sentences	-	Are any sentences too long?
	-	Are the sentences complete?
	-	Is the sentence length varied?
• Words	-	How is the spelling? Use a dictionary!
	-	Are slang and casual expressions avoided?
	-	Are there any unnecessary padding words that could be cut?
• Punctuation	-	(See Appendix C, p. 118.)
• Sexist Language	-	(See Appendix D, p. 125.)
• Referencing	-	(See Chapter 12, p. 99.)

4.8   Proofreading and Presentation

This is the time to polish your work; proofread your manuscript for:

- correctness   -   eliminate typographical errors and spelling mistakes; check your quotes
- format   -   is the manuscript visually attractive? (i.e. orderly, with obvious divisions and subdivisions – headings, subheadings, paragraphs.)
    -    does it invite readership? (i.e. type clear, line spacing correct, page numbers correct, headings and numbering system follow a consistent format.)
- quality   -   does the manuscript have the appearance of a professional document?

If possible, ask someone to proofread your assignment – they may spot errors you have missed.

4.9   Hand in the Assignment on Time – and Reward Yourself

You **deserve** it!

5. Research Reports

Much scientific writing follows a basic format. Research reports and scientific journal articles are all structured along similar lines. The **context** of a project (e.g. whether you are writing at elementary or advanced level, or whether your work involves original experimentation) will determine how much work goes into which sections, or whether to include or delete certain sections. A literature review, for example, would **NOT** be used at elementary levels.

The basic format is as follows:

Format of a Research Report

Title Page
Table of Contents (may be required for reports longer than six pages)
Abstract
Introduction (which may include a brief review of pertinent literature)
Literature Review (for advanced research assignments)
Materials and Methods
Results
Discussion
Conclusion
References
Appendices

Flexibility, according to the requirements of a particular lecturer or a particular assignment, is essential. This structure is a basic format to be adapted to suit the problem at hand, and to meet the needs of the reader. **If you have any doubt about the structure of a particular assignment, always consult the lecturer or tutor who set the assignment**.

The following pages describe the basic content of each section of a research report. Use these pages as a guide to mould each section of your work. Be prepared to rewrite the sections until you have conveyed your ideas or described your work clearly.

Remember that the purpose of any report is to convey an interpretation or findings in a particular situation to someone else. This should be done as clearly and succinctly as possible.

5.1 Title Page

The title page is the first page to appear in a report. It answers the question

What is the paper about?

It must contain the following information:

- The title of the report
- The name of the person or group **by whom** it is submitted
- The name of the person or group **to whom** it is submitted
- The date of submission
- Paper title and number

This information should be formatted as follows:

**Soil moisture deficit as a
predictor for dairy factory milk intake**

(16.9.04)

By: J. Massey-Smith
To: Dr I.M. Busy
Paper: 19.xxx Ag.Research

Figure 5.1:   Format of a Title Page

Titles should be short, specific and descriptive. They should contain the key words of the report in a way that captures the interest of the reader.

Example

Poor: Precipitation and evaporation influences on bovine lactation and the consequences for industrial dairy production planning.

Better: Soil moisture deficit as a predictor for dairy factory milk intake.

5.2   Table of Contents

A Table of Contents is used **only** in a lengthy research report (six pages or more). It should contain the most important headings and sub-headings which appear in the text of the report.

Page numbers should always be included, and checked for accuracy. The final

Figure 5.2: A Well-presented Table of Contents

copy of the Table of Contents should be made up **after** the report has been typed or written up in its final form to ensure that headings and page numbers are correct.

The Table of Contents is like an outline of the project, and guides the readers to information they wish to pursue. It should be accurate and presented in a neat, professional way.

List of Figures or Tables

If you are writing a lengthy report at an advanced level, and are using many illustrations (e.g. tables, photographs, diagrams), they should be given in a separate list on a separate page immediately after the Table of Contents page. This page should be headed List of Tables or List of Figures. NB: **A list of figures or tables is not necessary for undergraduate assignments**.

5.3 Abstract

An Abstract is used in longer reports, e.g. advanced research reports and scientific journal articles. It should be no longer than 300 words (is more commonly 150 words) and is centred on a separate page.

The abstract is not a preparatory section; rather, it is the report in miniature. Its purpose is to enable the reader to decide whether to read the rest of the report. It should be brief and informative. It should contain the following information:

1. Why the experiment was done (purpose)
2. How the experiment was carried out (method)
3. The main results
4. Any key conclusions drawn.

The abstract should be written in the past tense as a single paragraph. It MUST be self-contained; that is, the reader should not need to refer to parts of the report to understand the abstract: it should stand alone.

Abstract

Hand removal of weeds, predominantly white clover but also *Poa annua* L. and broad leaved species increased seed yield in a second-year lucerne crop from 0.7 to 21.3 g m^{-2} mainly because racemes increased from 89 to 1230 m^{-2}. Increases in pods per raceme and seeds per pod were also recorded. Hexazinone applied at 1.0 kg ai ha^{-1} during active vegetative growth in early spring eliminated white clover from the lucerne plots and increased seed yield to 14.3 g m^{-2}. However, this treatment did not control *Rumex obtusifolius* L. Simazine plus paraquat (2.25 kg ai plus 0.6 kg ai ha^{-1}) applied in winter before active spring growth controlled many annual weeds but, although initially checking white clover, did not control it. As a consequence, seed yield did not differ from that of the untreated control. Although hexazinone effectively removed white clover from a second-year lucerne seed crop, it is recommended for use only on mature stands. White clover removal from first year stands still requires investigation. Harvested lucerne seed viability did not differ among treatments, but hand weeding and herbicide treatments significantly reduced the percentage of hard seed.

Figure 5.3:   Example of an Abstract

5.4   Introduction

The main questions which should be answered in an Introduction are:

Why did you do the work?
What is its purpose?

An Introduction should be short, so try to answer these questions as simply and clearly as possible. You are aiming to interest the reader in your topic, to encourage them to read on, so lead them from information they already know to information they need to know. Introductions should contain the following:

1. The nature and scope of the problem investigated
2. A brief review of the pertinent literature
3. The reasons justifying the investigation (the hypothesis)
4. The objectives of the study.

Introduction

Weed control in forage lucerne (*Medicago sativa* L.) in New Zealand is well documented (Butler 1982; Palmer 1982; O'Connor 1990), but there is a dearth of research on weed control in crops grown for seed (Dunbier, Wynn-Williams and Purves 1983). However, a limited number of reports from other countries have shown that weed competition can significantly reduce lucerne seed yield. For example Waddington (1985) reported that control of primarily smooth brome (*Bromus inermis* Leyss.) increased seed yield by 68%, while Dawson & Rincker (1982) found that by keeping lucerne weed free, seed yield was 820 kg ha^{-1} compared with 45 kg ha^{-1} for the unweeded control.

While a large number of weed species can be present in lucerne seed crops in New Zealand, many can be successfully controlled by pre-sowing treatment with trifluralin (Butler 1982) and inter-row cultivation (Dunbier et al. 1983). However, two problem weeds are red clover (*Trifolium pratense* L.) and white clover (*Trifolium repens* L.), the former because seed size similarities can make this species difficult to clean from lucerne seed lots, and the latter because of the large plant population that can establish from volunteer-buried seed (Hampton, Clifford and Rolston 1987), leading to intense competition with the lucerne plants (Askarian 1993).

A second-year lucerne seed crop contained a heavy contamination from established white clover plants, and also a number of weed species including *Poa annua* L., dandelion (*Taraxacum officinale* Weber), twin cress (*Coronopus didymus* (L.) Sm.), annual mouse-ear chick-weed (*Cerastium glomeratum* Thuill) and broad-leaved dock (*Rumex obtusifolius* L.) (Askarian 1993). Simazine plus paraquat is commonly used for weed control in lucerne forage crops (Atkinson & Meeklah 1980), while Waddington (1985) reported that hexazinone could be successfully used for selective weed control in established lucerne seed crops. In New Zealand this herbicide is registered for use in established lucerne forage stands (O'Connor 1990) for the control of a number of weeds, including white clover. In this paper we report the effects of chemical and non-chemical control of white clover and other weeds on lucerne seed yield and quality.

Figure 5.4: Example of an Introduction

5.5   Full Literature Review

A full literature review (as opposed to a brief review of the literature included in an Introduction) is generally only used at very advanced levels. If you are writing a 100 or 200 level assignment **do not include a literature review unless you have specifically been asked to include one by your lecturer**.

If you have been asked to provide a literature review you need to consider the following points. The following guidelines are adapted from Brennan (1990).

A literature review is a summary of all the key research findings on a particular subject. It shows how your work relates to the research of other people; it puts your work in context.

As noted by Ary, Jacobs & Razavieh (1979, pp. 57–78), a literature review serves several important functions. It can be used:

(a) to enable the researcher to define the frontiers of the field
(b) to enable the researcher to develop an understanding of theory in that field and enable the research question to be placed in perspective
(c) to identify the procedures and instruments that have proved useful in the past and to identify those that seem less promising
(d) to avoid unintentional replication of previous studies
(e) to place the researcher in a better position to interpret the significance of the results obtained.

The purpose of basic or academic research is to extend and contribute to the current body of knowledge in a given field. It is therefore essential that the researcher is aware of and builds upon the work of others in the field. Ary, Jacobs & Razavieh (1979) suggest that, in a sense, the researcher should be saying:

> The work of A, B and C has discovered this much about my question; the investigations of D have added this much to our knowledge. I propose to go beyond D's work in the following manner (p. 57).

It is beyond the scope of this manual to describe the procedures involved in a literature search. Needless to say, a researcher must develop library skills and become familiar with bibliographic and abstract indexes and computer database facilities. As a start to this process, refer to Chapter 2, p. 12 on useful library sources.

Once you have located the literature in the field, it needs to be organised. A useful way to do this is to arrange the studies you have located into topics and then look at how each of these topics relates to your own study.

Your literature review should show what is already known and what remains to be investigated. Your hypothesis needs to relate to the past, and to future directions.

Do not present the literature review as a series of abstracts. Arrange your material according to ideas/themes/ topics rather than listing what each author says.

5.6   Materials and Methods

This section answers the following questions:

What materials did you use?
How did you use them?

It contains the following information:

> 1. The experimental design or theoretical approach
> 2. What materials were used in precise detail
> 3. What was done and how (method).

The purpose of this section is to provide enough information to allow an experienced colleague to repeat your experiment or assess how reliable your approach is. You must, therefore, be **accurate** and **precise**. Aim also to be concise – do not drown your materials and methods section in highly detailed but irrelevant description. Remember, too, that this section is being written for other specialists in the field, so widely accepted methods can be stated and appropriately referenced rather than described in great detail (unless, of course, your lecturer asks you to provide more detail).

Present the method section in a logical order – usually, describe events in the order in which they took place. If your work includes statistical analysis, state which method is used. Use subheadings if they will help the reader to understand and follow your work.

Never use personal pronouns in this section (i.e. I, we, you).

Write in the past tense.

Materials and Methods

The experiment was conducted at Massey University, Palmerston North, New Zealand (40°S 170°E) on an Ohakea silt loam soil classified as an aeric fragiaqualf (gleyed yellow-grey earth) with a pH of 5.2. The stand of lucerne cv. Grasslands Oranga had been established in 30 cm rows using a sowing rate of 3 kg ha⁻¹ in 1991 (Askarian & Hampton 1993) and a seed harvest taken in March 1992 (Askarian 1993). The stand was grazed to 7 cm on 30 July 1992. Honey bees (9 colonies ha^{-1}) were introduced to the trial area on 24 December 1992 to facilitate pollination.

A control (weeds undisturbed), two herbicide treatments and a hand weeding treatment were each replicated three times in a complete randomised block design. Plot size was 1.5 × 2 m. Simazine (2.25 kg ai ha^{-1}) plus paraquat (0.6 kg ai ha^{-1}) was applied on 30 August 1992 before active vegetative lucerne growth, while hexazinone (1.0 kg ai ha^{-1}) was applied on 30 September 1992 during active weed growth (O'Connor 1990). Herbicides were applied via a small gas pressure sprayer in 400 litre water ha^{-1} at 200 kPa. Hand weeding was begun on 30 September 1992 and continued at two-weekly intervals until February 1993.

Figure 5.5: One Subsection of a Materials and Method Section

5.7 Results

The Results section answers the following question:

What did you find or see?

All the results that will appear in the report **must** be presented in the Results section – no results should appear for the first time in, for example, the Discussion or Conclusion.

You will have to decide which results to include and how best to present them. Focus on the results which relate to your hypothesis or objectives. Put key results at the top of paragraphs or into subsections so that they are clearly evident to the reader. Decide on a logical order for the subsections so that they follow naturally from one another – one good way to do this is to structure the results in the same order as your objectives.

Results should be presented in a clear and objective way so that the readers can draw their own conclusions from them. They **must** therefore be concise and accurate. Check all figures to ensure their accuracy.

Sometimes, if you are not going to discuss your findings in detail, you may choose to combine the Results and Discussion sections. In this case, briefly state what your findings mean as you present them.

Always explain the significance of a table or figure – and make sure all graphics are given a label and a title. Avoid wordy descriptions of data that are already apparent to the reader from examination of the figure or tables; perhaps emphasise the main points (briefly) but do not put the graph or table into words and hence present your results twice.

Results

At 1 November 1992 total percentage ground cover was greatest for the unweeded control, followed by the two herbicides treatments, with the hand weeding treatment having only just over one third ground cover (Table 1). However, for the control, only 13% of this cover was lucerne with white clover constituting 60% and other weed species 26% of the cover. Hand weeding and the herbicide treatments significantly increased the percentage of lucerne as plant ground cover (Table 1), and significantly decreased the percentage of white clover compared with unweeded plots, although hexazinone and hand weeding were more effective than simazine plus paraquat (Table 1).

By 1 February 1993, both of the herbicide treatments and hand weeding had increased (P < 0.05) the percentage of lucerne in the plant cover (Table 1). The hexazinone application and hand weeding had eliminated white clover from the plant cover but there was no significant difference in the white clover cover of the unweeded plots and those treated with simazine and paraquat (Table 1). Other weeds (Table 1) still present included twin cress, dandelion, broad-leaved dock and annual mouse-ear chickweed.

Figure 5.6: One Subsection of a Results Section

5.8   Discussion

The Discussion section must answer the general question

What do your findings mean?

The following are features of a good discussion:

- First, **discuss**. Do not recapitulate the results. Instead, try to present the principles and relationships shown by the results.
- Point out any exceptions or lack of correlation. Do not try to 'fudge' to cover up data that do not quite fit.
- For advanced level reports, compare (or contrast) your results with previously published work.
- Discuss what your results mean in relation to the initial hypothesis or objectives.
- Consider the relevance, usefulness and limitations of your study. Be honest. If you recognise a problem/limitation, say so.
- Be careful that you do not get carried away with sweeping generalisations or unsubstantiated speculation. Remember the results of one pasture trial in one region are not relevant to all farmers across the country, so rein in your enthusiasm.

The main parts of the discussion should be presented in order of importance – or in the same order as the main points in the Results section and objectives (ideally, both alternatives should come together). Do not be tempted to start with insignificant points and build up to your main point; state the main points early, and each main point **at the beginning** of a paragraph, so that the reader can easily locate the key points made. (For more detail on paragraphing, see Appendix C, p. 115.)

For Advanced Level Projects Only

Discussion

Competition from weeds resulted in an 82% reduction in total lucerne dry matter production because when compared with hand weeded plots, racemes m^{-2} were reduced by over 90%. The net effect of this for seed production was a 97% reduction in seed yield due to the presence of weeds, a result very similar to the 95% reduction reported by Dawson & Rincker (1982). Initially at this site, most of this weed competition came from white clover (Table 1), but as the season progressed other weed species including dandelion, broad leaved dock, twin cress and annual mouse-ear chickweed also became important. However, by final harvest the major weed component was still white clover. White clover plants reached their maximum height in January and began to lodge, forcing the lucerne plants to lodge as well. This occurred during lucerne flowering, and it is possible that in addition to the competition for light, nutrients and water provided by the weeds, lodged lucerne flowers were less accessible to pollinators.

Figure 5.7:   One Subsection of a Discussion

Show how your findings relate to other work in the field (i.e. make connections with your literature review). State or show what is new in your work and why your results are important – how they add to the body of knowledge on the subject – but do not make your claims too extravagant!

5.9   Conclusion

The Conclusion should "wrap up" the report by summarising the major points made in the Discussion in relation to your hypothesis. It should be kept short and to the point. Avoid banal statements such as "This study has pointed to some interesting implications for research in the field". Statements like these add nothing of use or interest to the reader.

It may be relevant to some studies to end with a list or short discussion of specific recommendations for directions of further research.

Conclusion

Failure to control weeds, predominantly white clover, but also broad leaved species, decreased the seed yield of a second year lucerne crop by 92%. Applying hexazinone at 1.0 kg ai ha^{-1} in early spring killed white clover, and lucerne seed yield was significantly increased. However, there is a problem in that hexazinone is only recommended for use on mature lucerne stands, and whether this herbicide can be safely used for white clover control in first year stands is yet to be determined.

Figure 5.8:   An Example of an Effective Conclusion

5.10   References

Every report that draws on other people's ideas or findings must have a reference section where sources are cited in full.

The reference **lists all the sources that have been cited in the report**. In other words, if you have sources but have not cited them, they should not appear in your References. If you have sources which have been influential but not cited, they should be listed under the heading Bibliography, and should immediately follow your list of references.

For detailed discussion on formatting the References and Bibliography see Chapter 12, p. 100.

5.11 Appendices

Material that is complex and/or detailed is collected at the end of the report in the appendices section so as not to distract readers from the main theme.

Appendices may contain supplementary illustrative material which a reader may want to refer to after they have read the report, for example, questionnaires, letters, pamphlets which illustrate some aspects of the material discussed in the text.

Appendices are also useful to relegate detailed explanations of a model or theoretical approach referred to in the discussion. If some specialist readers – but not **most** readers – would want certain material, it should be placed in an appendix.

Appendices should always be presented in a professional manner, so do not be tempted to just fold up all your computer print-out figures and staple them to the end of your report! You still need to organise and select material and present it in a way that is easily understood by your reader. Appendices should always be given a number or letter, and title:

Appendix A: Map of the Manawatu Region
or Appendix 1: Supply Figures 1999–2004

When referring to an Appendix in the body of a report, explain its significance. Do not just add "Refer to Appendices 1, 3 and 7" to the end of a sentence. Rather, explain to the reader how the appendix will be of use to them, e.g. "Refer to Appendix A for a more detailed description of this model".

Appendices should:

- provide detailed explanation serving the needs of some specialised readers
- be clearly and neatly set out
- be numbered (or lettered)
- be given a title
- be arranged in the order that they are mentioned in the text
- be related to the report's objectives and not just 'tacked on'.

---

6. Report to a Client

A report to a client (or business report) differs markedly, in structure and style, to a research report. The purpose of a business report is generally more focused on a practical context and its audience is often a specific person with a specific concern or problem. Lecturers usually set business reports at undergraduate level so students can:

- develop and demonstrate an understanding of a concept or theory
- develop and demonstrate the ability to relate this theory or concept to a practical situation.

The basic format of a business report is as follows:

Format of a Business Report
Letter or Memo to the client
Title Page
Table of Contents (for reports longer than six pages)
Introduction
Background
Discussion
Conclusions
Recommendations (if appropriate)
References
Appendices

This format should be adopted to suit the context, purpose and audience of the report. A Recommendations section, for example, is only appropriate where the purpose of the report is to deal with a problem or where indications for future direction are requested. Be flexible and adapt your report to suit the needs of your reader. If you are in doubt about the structure of your report, always consult with the person who set the assignment.

The rest of this chapter describes the basic content of each section of a business report. There are **conventions** relating to what goes into each section. The purpose of these conventions is to save the reader's time. If the reader just wants to know what the key findings are, for example, they do not have to flick through the whole report: they can turn immediately to the covering letter or Conclusions. If they want to know the purpose of the report, they can go straight to the Introduction. Use these pages, then, as a guide to mould each section of your work. Be prepared to rewrite your sections until you are confident that you have conveyed your ideas clearly to your reader.

Remember that the purpose of your report is not just to complete your analysis. Reports are requested when someone has a particular need for specific information. Communicating your ideas, findings and the interpretation of results from analyses is vitally important. Express your ideas clearly and present them professionally.

6.1 Covering Letter or Memo

If the report is written for a receiver outside your organisation, a covering letter should be attached; if the report is for a reader within your organisation, a memorandum (memo) is the appropriate format. Basically, the covering note passes the report over officially from writer to reader. It reminds the reader(s) of the terms of reference agreed upon for the report, courteously acknowledges any assistance and expresses willingness to supply more help. If you are writing to a single individual you would also include your key findings.

A covering letter or memo must be formatted professionally. It is expected that you will submit a professionally correct letter or memo, as laid out below:

Aims of a Covering Letter or Memo

The covering letter or memo should:
- identify the report topic, and scope or extent of the investigation
- identify the person who authorised the report, and the date of authorisation
- communicate key findings
- acknowledge any assistance in preparation of the report
- indicate willingness to provide further information.

MEMORANDUM

TO:	J R Farron, Director
FROM:	J M Clarke, Research Advisor
DATE:	16 September 2004
SUBJECT:	Financial Plan – Mr and Mrs Stuart

Please find enclosed the report requested by you on the management plan for Mr and Mrs Stuart. My brief was to prepare a financial management plan for the 2004/05 season for situations where the existing horticultural operation was maintained and where a neighbouring 10 ha property with 3–5-year-old apple trees was purchased.

1. The forecast cashflow budgets for the existing and expanded orchard businesses were based on current levels of production and MAF Policy forecasted prices (May 2004) for various apple varieties and grades.

2. Total production of apples would increase by 30,000 tray carton equivalents (100%) if the neighbouring orchard was acquired. These would be produced between March and May.

3. The net cash surplus would increase by 120% to $60,000 with the expanded operation. Economies of scale for labour and machinery, and a better varietal mix (20% more Braeburn) would contribute to the proportionately greater returns.

4. It is recommended that arrangements to purchase the property proceed forthwith. It will be necessary to arrange a 10-year loan of $100,000 to purchase the land and buildings.

Figure 6.1:   Format for a Memo Introducing a Report

AgriBus Consultants
PO Box 994
Palmerston North

16 September 2004

Mr & Mrs Stuart
"Takitaki" R D 3
Hawkes Bay

Dear Mr & Mrs Stuart

Please find enclosed the financial management plan requested by you on 14 July 2004. Our brief was to prepare a financial management plan for the 2004/05 season for situations where the existing horticultural operation was maintained and where a neighbouring 10 ha property with 3–5-year-old apple trees was purchased.

1. The forecast cashflow budget for the existing and expanded orchard businesses was based on current levels of production and MAF Policy forecast prices (May 2004) for various apple varieties and grades.

2. Total production of apples would increase by 30,000 tray carton equivalents (100%) if the neighbouring orchard was acquired. These would be produced between March and May.

3. The net cash surplus would increase by 120% to $60,000 with the expanded operation. Economies of scale for labour and machinery, and a better varietal mix (20% more Braeburn) would contribute to the proportionately greater returns.

4. It is recommended that arrangements to purchase the property proceed forthwith. It will be necessary to arrange a 10-year loan of $100,000 to purchase the land and buildings.

If you need any further information, please feel free to contact me. I would be happy to investigate whether the potential expenditure savings identified earlier can be realised.

Yours sincerely

J M Clarke
AgriBus Consultant

Figure 6.2:   Format of a Business Letter Introducing a Report

6.2 Title Page

The title page states the report's title. It should be focused and brief, but descriptive enough for the report to be filed appropriately. The title should be positioned by itself about a third of the way down the page surrounded by white space. The date the report was completed should be placed under the title, and your name and the name of the person it is submitted to with the paper name and number in the bottom corner of the page. A relevant icon (e.g. from a word processing package), strategically placed, can improve the visual appeal of the title page.

**Business management plan
for Elderfarm**

(19.8.04)

By: K O'Connor
To: Dr B Stuart
Paper: 11.xxx Farm Management II

Figure 6.3:   Format of a Title Page

Make your title specific and focused.

> **Examples**
>
> Poor: A report on financial management of "Takitaki."
>
> Better: Report to Mr & Mrs Stuart on a financial plan for "Takitaki" during 2004/05.

6.3   Table of Contents

If the report is longer than six pages, a Table of Contents helps to orient readers to the scope and emphases in the report. It also gives the page number for the beginning of each section. The headings of each section and sub-section should be identical to those which appear in the report. The logical relationship between the sections may be signalled by numbering, indentation or font size and upper/lower case, or a combination of these methods.

For an example of a Table of Contents see p. 36, Research Reports.

6.4   Introduction

The Introduction should lead readers from information they already know and share with you, the writer, to information they need to acquire. Begin with a general overview statement that identifies the subject matter of the report and establishes common ground with the readers. Then state the change, problem or issue which has brought about the need for the investigation reported here. It is often helpful to present this 'change, problem or issue' in terms of a question which your report will help answer. In some situations it may be useful to state the terms of reference in the Introduction so that the reader knows the specific areas which are to be addressed in the report. Define the report's objectives precisely, and in terms that would interest your specific readers.

Having given the 'big picture' and then focused on the issues to be explored in this report, do not keep readers in suspense. Your report is always written because someone has a question. Summarise very briefly here your answer to the question addressed by this report. The next section will expand your conclusions in more detail.

Besides introducing the issues your report will discuss, this section should also clarify what readers can expect from the report. Indicate the scope of the report. If evaluation or judgement is involved, set out your criteria for evaluating alternatives. It is also good practice to preview the report's structure, indicating how you have grouped your material and in what sequence you will present it.

In the world of business and science, report writers frequently comment in the report on its limitations. Even though you are writing as a student, it may occasionally be appropriate to caution readers about the variables affecting your conclusions and recommendations, for example, limited resources or time, or assumptions which you had to make.

Writing an Introduction

The Introduction should:

- identify the general subject matter and context
- describe the change, problem or issue to be reported on
- define the specific objectives for this report
- indicate the overall answer to the query explored in the report
- outline the scope of the report (extent of investigation)
- set out criteria for evaluation (if analytical report)
- preview the report structure
- comment on the limitations of this report and any assumptions made.

Introduction

The Blacklers purchased their 700 ha sheep and beef cattle farm "Tainui" in 1988. At takeover the farm wintered 5000 breeding ewes, 1000 ewe hoggets and 200 Angus breeding cows or the equivalent of 10.0 su per hectare. However, lamb and wool production by the Perendale flock purchased with the property has been poor. Lambing percentages averaged only 75% and wool production per ewe was 2.8 kg/year between 1989 and 1993. As a consequence, sheep returns are only 50% of the district average.

The Blacklers therefore asked Agribus Consultants to investigate strategies that would improve sheep productivity and returns. This was to include a review of the whole farming operation and was to particularly focus on the grazing management applied to the flock replacements. Alternative sheep enterprises that involved fine woolled breeds (<30 microns) were not to be considered.

This report presents the results of the whole farm feed budget analysis and the gross margins for six alternative ewe breeding and lamb finishing systems. A liveweight profile for flock replacements to reach 55 kg at mating is presented and suggested management policies are outlined.

Figure 6.4: Example of an Introduction

6.5 Background

The background section of a business report sets out a full and relevant description of the subject which you are analysing. It "sets the scene" for the analysis. The description should be limited to those factors which are relevant to the type of analysis you have been asked to conduct.

Present your material in subject blocks, perhaps using sub-headings. Deal with one subject at a time. Present these sections in a logical order in relation to the objectives of your report.

Most specialist reports to farmer clients will include a property description within the background section. The objective of the property description is to concisely describe the property, identify key resources, particularly those that may limit farm productivity and profitability, and define the goals and objectives of the farmer (and the farmer's family).

A property description should be completed in approximately 1–1½ pages in most undergraduate reports and each paragraph should group related topics from the three resource headings, Land, Labour and Capital. These may be grouped as follows:

1. Farmer/ownership and topography of the farm
2. Labour resources and farmer objectives
3. Climate/soils including fertiliser and drainage
4. Subdivision/pastures and water supply
5. Stock and performance (physical)
6. Buildings and machinery.

Background

The farm owned by Mr and Mrs John Blatchard is a 50 hectare (ha) seasonal supply dairy farm. It is situated 10 km south-east of Palmerston North on flat to gently rolling country. The primary objective of the Blatchards is to run an efficient commercial operation maximising profit from the land. In addition, the owners aim to have at least 3 weeks holiday with the family during the summer. Mr and Mrs Blatchard run the farm, with some casual assistance from their two teenage children. Silage is made by contractors, and some outside casual labour is also hired as required.

cont....

Figure 6.5:   **Example of an Effective Background Section**

The soil type is Tokomaru silt loam, a medium fertility soil with poor natural drainage. To overcome the drainage problem the farm has been intensively tile and mole drained. Two feed pads are also used in the winter to minimise pugging by the herd. The average rainfall is 1000 mm per year and this is fairly evenly distributed. However, the farm normally experiences a dry spell during February and March and this can be exacerbated by the hot, dry winds that prevail from the west.

The property is subdivided into 24 paddocks with 2–3 wire electric fences and has good race access. The water is supplied to troughs in each paddock by a 40 millimetre (mm) ring main. The pastures are predominantly ryegrass and white clover and receive 350 kg/ha of thirty per cent potassic longlife superphosphate each autumn.

In 1992 the farm wintered 154 Friesian-Jersey crossbred cows. The 40 replacement heifers are grazed off from May to May. This season the farm is expected to produce 270 kilograms (kg) of milksolids (MS) per cow and 800 kg MS/ha. This is only slightly above the district average despite the good pasture-growing season.

The farm has a 14-a-side herringbone shed, associated oxidation ponds and calf rearing sheds. Other buildings on the farm include a 4 bedroom house, 2000 bale capacity hay shed and small implement shed. The machinery on the property includes a tractor (80 kW) and cultivation equipment, silage wagon and a four-wheel motorcycle.

6.6   Discussion

This is the main body of the report. It should be subdivided into logical units, each with an informative heading drawn from the subject matter that follows.

Sometimes the aim of a report is merely to describe a situation or some data. More often, you need to analyse the data, drawing out the implications in terms of your objectives. In this section you provide the evidence that supports the document's main conclusions and which justifies your recommendation. The evidence you supply may be in the form of specific instances, relevant theories, research findings, statistics, or expert's testimony. This evidence will come from your analysis of data, reading, discussion with peers, and reflection on the report's subject. Do not present the evidence as if it speaks for itself; use the evidence to support a point you want to make, and report it as briefly as possible.

If the problem is complex, you may want to consider the problem from different perspectives – each angle implying different solutions.

Novice report writers sometimes wander away from the objectives stated in the

Introduction. Keep the reader's problem – what he or she needs to know to understand the issue and, perhaps, make a decision – firmly in mind while writing this section.

The Discussion section often includes graphics and tabular support for the main points made. See Chapter 9, p. 75 for some suggestions on how to develop clear figures and tables.

NB: The major purpose of this section is to explain your conclusions and justify your recommendations.

Writing the Discussion

The Discussion section should:

- be subdivided into logical units, each with a heading
- present units in a logical sequence
- present and debate the evidence which supports the conclusions
- justify the recommendations
- present only material focused on the report's objectives
- illustrate main points where possible with graphics or tables.

6.7   Conclusions

The Conclusions section of a report summarises the key findings which have been presented in the Discussion. These are presented as a list of numbered points which highlight crucial problem areas or issues to be considered by the reader. The Conclusions should relate directly to the objectives or terms of reference laid out in the Introduction.

Writing a Conclusion

The Conclusions should:

- relate specifically to the objectives for the report set out in the Introduction
- follow logically from the facts in the Discussion
- be clear-cut and specific
- be arranged so that the major conclusions come first
- be short (full explanation is given in the Discussion section)
- identify the major issues relating to the case.

Conclusions

Alternative calving dates (15 July or 1 August) for the Lovelock property were compared in terms of their effect on annual milksolids production and financial returns. The feed budget analysis showed:

1. That the present calving date should be maintained. Milksolids production could be improved further if a more condensed calving pattern was achieved through improved cow nutrition in early lactation.

2. Average pasture cover with the early-calving system would fall to 900 kg DM/ha in the first week of August if no nitrogen or extra supplements were used.

3. To maintain a minimum target pasture cover of 1600 kg DM/ha during August and September it would be necessary to apply 100 kg urea/ha during the first week of July and to achieve a response of 10.0 kg DM/kg N applied (or to feed out 5000 bales of hay). It is highly unlikely that this level of nitrogen response will be achieved in a year when average weather conditions occur.

4. The farm surplus would be reduced by $50/ha if the early-calving option with extra nitrogen fertiliser inputs was adopted, or $75/ha if extra hay was purchased for the spring period.

Figure 6.6:   Example of an Effective Conclusions Section

6.8   Recommendations

While conclusions are objectively derived from the evidence provided in the Discussion, Recommendations are the subjective opinions of the writer about what course of action should be followed. But subjectivity does not mean anything goes. They should take into account such issues as cost, location and acceptability relative to current policy or practice.

The reader should also be prepared for the Recommendations by material presented in the Discussion section. They should not come 'out of the blue'.

Note that not all reports have Recommendations. They are only included in reports which aim to specify a course of action.

Writing Recommendations

Recommendations should:

- be feasible
- be related logically to the Discussion and Conclusions
- be numbered where there are several recommendations
- be arranged in order of importance.

6.9   References

Every report that draws on other people's ideas or findings must have a reference section where sources are cited in full.

The purpose of the reference section is to **list all the sources cited in the report**; if you have sources but have not cited them, they should not appear in your References. Sources which have been influential but not cited, should be listed under the heading Bibliography and should immediately follow your list of references.

For detailed discussion on formatting References and Bibliography see Chapter 12, p. 100.

6.10   Appendices

For a detailed description of what to include in Appendices and directions on presentation see p. 46.

6.11   Student Model

To view a full example of a student written report to a client, see Appendix F.

7. Essays

Essays are not used often as assignments in an applied science course. The most common situation where essays are required is in **exams**. This chapter of the Writing Guidelines considers essays in general. Students preparing for exam essays should read both this chahpter and Appendix E, p. 127: Exam Skills.

Essays require some very specific skills. They require the student to acquire and assess a range of information in the light of a particular question. This means students must distinguish between different sorts of information, evaluate what others have said and then formulate their own ideas in the context of these different perspectives. Finally, ideas must be presented in such a way that the reader knows that the student understands the debate on a particular topic and can logically present a case for a specific perspective on the topic.

7.1   Essay Structure

Essays have a remarkably simple structure compared with reports. In English teachers' jargon, the structure of an essay is the statement and logical defence of a proposition. Put more simply, this means that an essay states a key point – or series of points – (a proposition) in its introduction. The body of the essay then explains why these key points are so – what evidence supports your point? It may also consider why the opposing position(s) is weak. What figures, facts and ideas can be used to defend this perspective? Then, at the end, the essay summarises the main supporting evidence and restates the key point, the proposition. The diagram on page 54 shows this basic structure.

Usually the essay is set out as a single unit without headings; however, some lecturers or markers may like headings. The general rule to follow is this:

> Do not use headings in essays unless you have been specifically directed to do so.

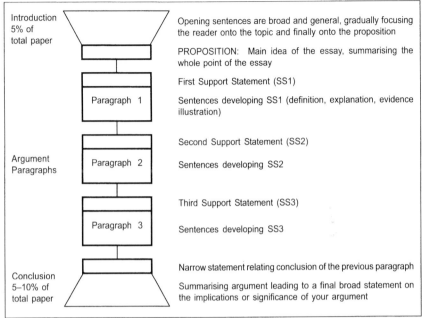

Figure 7.1: Basic Essay Structure

(Source Unknown)

1. *Introductions*

Introductions usually start with broad and general statements about the topic and become gradually more focused until you state your key points at the end of the Introduction. You might begin with some background information, a question, dilemma or paradox, or an eye-catching quotation. Avoid starting with dictionary definitions, a restatement of the topic or the utterly boring "The purpose of this essay is to prove that ...". Aim to interest your reader in the topic.

> Remember, your key idea(s), your proposition, should be placed at the end of your introduction. An essay is not like a short story – it does **not** require a surprise ending. Your reader wants to know exactly what you are talking about.

2. Body

The body of the essay is made up of paragraphs. Each paragraph is a single building block in the construction of the essay. Each paragraph should contain a single idea. The key idea of each paragraph should be situated **at the beginning** of the paragraph (the topic sentence), with the rest of the paragraph supporting, defending and explaining that idea. See p. 115 for more on paragraphing.

> Do not forget to consider all the evidence **against** your case. Explain why you have, nevertheless, decided to support **your** proposition.

3. Conclusions

The Conclusion should summarise the supporting evidence and restate the key point(s). It is often appropriate to widen the perspective in the final paragraph, showing how the study has implications for further research. However, do not introduce any new ideas at this stage – the Conclusion's main purpose is to sum up.

7.2 The Essay Writing Process

Figure 7.2 on page 61 shows two methods that can be used in writing essays.

1. Select the Question

If you have been given a selection of essay topics to choose from, pick one well in advance of the due completion date. Consider the following in making your choice:

- Which of the topics is most interesting?
- Which would be easiest?
- Which would be most useful? (Writing an essay on some topics may help you understand better certain important sections of the course you are doing. You may also suspect that questions are more likely to be asked on some topics than others in the final exam.)

2. Question the Question

Spend some time making sure that you comprehend the essay question. Make sure to:

- Be very clear on what the question requires. (What is it asking you to do? Have a look at instruction words, and the central terms and concepts given.)

- Think about what you already know of the topic, and what you still have to find out to be able to answer the question well. (It helps to write these down.)
- Identify important issues, either stated or implied in the question, that you will (or may) have to deal with in the essay.

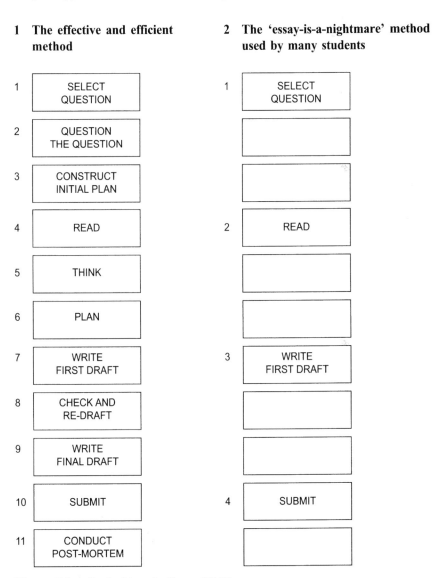

1 The effective and efficient method

1. SELECT QUESTION
2. QUESTION THE QUESTION
3. CONSTRUCT INITIAL PLAN
4. READ
5. THINK
6. PLAN
7. WRITE FIRST DRAFT
8. CHECK AND RE-DRAFT
9. WRITE FINAL DRAFT
10. SUBMIT
11. CONDUCT POST-MORTEM

2 The 'essay-is-a-nightmare' method used by many students

1. SELECT QUESTION
2. READ
3. WRITE FIRST DRAFT
4. SUBMIT

Figure 7.2: Basic Steps in Essay Writing

3. *Construct an Initial Essay Plan*

As far as is possible, try to decide what to include in your essay, and how it will be structured. It is very important to have planned the broad structure of the essay before moving on to the information gathering (reading) phase. (The only exception is when you really know very little about the topic – in which case, you may have to do some initial browsing beforehand.)

- Jot down headings and other ideas, and link them to indicate how they may relate to one another in your essay.
- From the plan, make a list of questions that you need to find answers for (e.g. What is the definition of ...? What characteristics of ... enable it to survive well in its environment? What important points does this highlight about plant adaptation? etc.). This list of questions will serve as your 'reading plan'.

4. *Read Selectively*

A reading plan is important when you start your research because it will help you read selectively and purposefully, rather than indiscriminately and without direction. This is the information gathering phase.

- Read material relevant to your essay plan, and to answer questions in your 'reading plan'.
- When necessary, modify your initial plan to take account of insights you get from reading.
- Take notes – but selectively. Do not rewrite whole sections of textbooks and other reading materials, jot down notes only on what will be useful for the essay. Try to use your own words as much as possible.
- If you need to use a quotation, copy it down accurately (including its source).
- Jot down information you will need for your References or Bibliography section now while you still have the books and other reading materials with you.

5. *Think*

This is a step that many students skip. Thinking is important if you want to reduce the likelihood of getting stuck later when you are writing.

- Stand off and assess the information you have gathered.
- It might be helpful to talk with others about the ideas and concepts of your essay, and reading material. Ask questions if necessary.

- Make sure you are clear about the answer you have decided upon, and the major points in your essay.

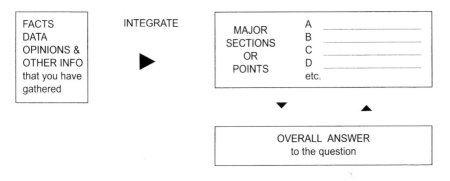

Figure 7.3:   Essay Plan

6. *Plan a Revised Essay Structure*

An essay basically consists of three parts:

- The Introduction: where you briefly describe what the essay will be about.
- The Main Body: where you make your points and assertions backed by evidence.
- The Conclusion/Summary: where you briefly sum up what you wrote about in your essay, and state any conclusions you drew from your study.

At this stage, it is very important to:

- Make a detailed plan of the Main Body of the essay. (If you prefer, you can sort out the Introduction and the Conclusion/Summary at a later stage.)
- Try to make sure that this plan is adequately detailed. It ideally should consist of a paragraph-by-paragraph outline of the points and assertions you wish to make and their supporting evidence, explanations, and/or arguments.

7. *Write the First Draft*

Use your plan to write an essay which analyses, synthesises and evaluates your ideas on the topic. Use the following as a guide to help you express your ideas clearly:

- Make your main point in the first sentence of a paragraph. The following sentences should then elaborate on, support, explain, and/or argue for that point.
- Put main and important points in paragraphs of their own.
- If you get stuck in writing down your thoughts: (i) consult your plan, (ii) clarify in your mind the specific point you want to make, (iii) think aloud or vocalise your ideas – as if you are explaining it to someone else, (iv) once it sounds good enough, write it down, (v) once you have written it down, you can then improve the sentence structure and/or clarify if necessary.

8. *Check and Re-draft*

After you have written the first draft of the essay, leave it for a day (if time allows) or overnight – so that it can be examined from a fresh perspective during the checking and re-drafting stage. Edit the essay for irrelevancy, excessive length, and faulty logic or grammar. Make sure that:

- The essay is not excessively lengthy and over the word limit.
- You have clearly answered the question given.
- You have kept to the topic, and excluded irrelevant points and unnecessary padding.
- The main ideas/points are clearly distinguished in separate paragraphs or sections.
- There is a logical sequence to the points in the essay.
- Every sentence is grammatical and easy to understand.
- Important or contentious terms are adequately explained and/or defined.
- There is enough evidence to support your claims or generalisations.
- You have written the essay in a reasonably interesting manner, and you have avoided being too wordy or repetitious.

If you have not done so yet, write the Introduction and Conclusion/Summary of your essay.

9. *Write the Final Draft*

Note the following points:

- Type the essay if possible. Use double-spacing.
- If you write it by hand, make sure that it is neat and readable.
- Make sure there are adequate margins on your pages.
- Be familiar with and comply with the documentation and format requirements

of your department and lecturers.
- Do not forget your References or Bibliography!
- Ask someone to proofread your work.

10. *Submit the Essay*

Even if you are not totally happy with the essay, submit it. If you do not submit anything, you will get a zero.

Make sure you provide clear identification of the assignment, course, your name, ID number, and other requested information on the cover page.

11. *Conduct a Post-mortem on the Essay*

When the essay has been marked and returned to you:

- Read and think about the marker's comments.
- Note the good points, and maybe errors, that you have made.
- Try to learn from the feedback you receive: to gain a better understanding of the concepts and issues involved, and to improve on subsequent essays.
- Make an appointment with your marker if necessary, to discuss and/or clarify points in the essay.

8. Business Writing

Business writing differs in many ways from most assignment writing. Assignments are mainly focused on the writer; business writing (letters, memos, reports) focuses on the reader: the reader's needs and abilities. Assignments are (more often than not) a form of evaluation; business writing is a vital form of communication. The worst that can happen if you write a shoddy assignment is that you may fail a paper or a course; poor writing in a business context may lead to loss of contracts, loss of income – and worse.

This section focuses on three forms of writing: memos, letters and CVs.

8.1   Memos

Memos are used as a form of communication **within** an organisation. They are formatted as outlined in Figure 8.1.

Try not to take a 'me'-centred approach to persuasion.

MEMORANDUM

TO: Michael Johanason
            Production Manager
FROM: Karen Hamlin
            Assistant Production Manager
DATE: 26 September 2004
SUBJECT: Failure to Meet Production Deadlines
            – A Solution

The present chronic inability of our production team to meet deadlines would, I believe, be alleviated by adding an evening roster to the processing schedule.

Since the demand for our product has increased, we have not been able to meet production deadlines. This has been a consistent problem for the last 9 months. Efforts to increase efficiency with the present processing system have led to only partial success in meeting deadlines. Staff have been pushed to their limits and I have heard talk of processors approaching the unions. Our present system is stretched almost beyond its capacity.

An evening roster would allow us to meet the needs of our customers without the costs of investing in new technology or plant. Under the new contracts, labour costs are very competitive and would not eat into profit margins.

I have worked through the figures and would be happy to discuss my findings with you further.

Figure 8.1:   Memorandum Written in a Deductive Style

The message is stated under the subject line. There are two main ways of formatting the message: deductive and itemised.

Deductive

Because memos tend to be brief (they are usually written for and by busy people), the main idea or the main purpose of the memo can be placed in the opening sentence and then the rest of the memo can be used to provide justification or explanation for the opening statement. The advantage of this approach is that it is a very clear way of writing, and the reader will not miss the purpose of the memo.

Itemised

An itemised approach is practical when a series of points are to be made which are equally important. Each point should be numbered, and deal with a separate issue.

MEMORANDUM

TO: Jane Burrows, Personal Assistant
FROM: Rose O'Connor, Manager
DATE: 21 March 2004
SUBJECT: Growers Conference 16–19 Sept 2005

Please arrange the following for the conference:

1. Accommodation for 160 from 15–20 September. The conference goers need mid-range accommodation, close to town, with standard features. Accommodation should be within walking distance of the conference venue.

2. The conference venue is booked. Check that the facility has available:

    (i) Large conference room to seat 250.
    (ii) Eight smaller rooms for discussion groups and presentations.
    (iii) Presentation facilities in each presentation room and in the large conference room.

3. We are anticipating up to 80 day registrations per day. Book lunch and afternoon tea for 250 for each day.

4. On the 19th we have scheduled a day of visits to nearby properties. Check arrangements and arrange transportation.

5. Bring detailed costs to me by the end of the month.

Figure 8.2:   Memorandum Written in an Itemised Style

Whichever format you choose to use, you should employ a style which is clear and concise. Don't waste words, don't aim for elegant, mellifluous prose – make sure every word counts. You should aim to get your message across quickly and accurately.

8.2   Letters

Letters are the most common method of communicating formally to people outside your own organisation. Business letters, like memos, follow quite structured formatting conventions.

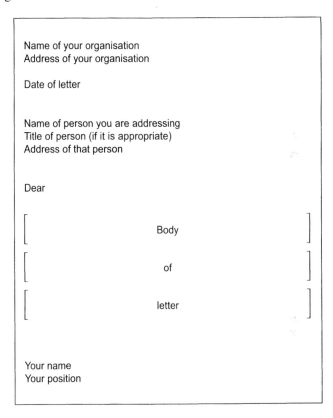

Figure 8.3:   Format of a Business Letter

Note that **everything** is justified from the left-hand margin and that paragraphs are not indented but separated by a double space.

Before you begin writing your letter, think about who you are writing to. Remember that you are writing to a person. What do you know about them? What do they know about you? What do you want them to do or understand in response to your letter? How can you write your letter so that you best achieve the desired response?

It is important that you take the time to think about this person before you write, especially if you want to persuade the reader to do something they might not naturally do (e.g. pay a bill, give you an interview for a job). Many new graduates, for example, write letters of application which basically say "I think you should employ me because it would be a great start for my career". Why should an employer want to do you a favour? Instead, you need to look at the application from the **reader's** perspective – what do they need that you can give? The message of a letter of application should be "I think you should employ me because I have precisely the skills your organisation needs".

The structure of a business letter is as follows:

- State the point of the letter immediately. Your reader is busy and will want to know immediately why they are reading this.
- Some context – you might need to explain the background or context of the letter, why it is being written.
- Explain any important facts relating to the main point.
- State what action, if any, is required.
- Close courteously.

If memos should be written in a concise and clear style, then we need to add another adjective to describe the style required in letters. A letter should be written in a style which is clear, concise and courteous. A letter writing style should not be overly brusque or clipped.

8.3 CVs (Curriculum Vitae)

A curriculum vitae is "a summary of your personal details, background, experience, skills and qualifications" (Elder, 1994, p. 250). Its aim is to give a prospective employer an impression of the scope of your abilities and achievements. It is generally accompanied by a list of referees who can flesh out the details of the CV.

While you are a student and when you are looking for work, you should always have, on disk or in a file, a generic or "all purpose" CV which you can modify for different jobs and different contexts. Keeping your generic CV on disk is an excellent idea, because then you can modify it easily to suit varying circumstances.

A CV should contain the following information. Remember to keep the details concise and specific.

1. *Personal Details*

Ideally personal details will be laid out to cover the first page. Include the following:

- full name
- home address
- telephone number (home and work – including STD number)
- date of birth
- health (this is optional, but if you are a non-smoker and exercise regularly, it may count in your favour, so you might mention this)
- career objective(s): these should be highlighted in some way – perhaps by placing them in a box. Be concise.

These are the details you would include on the first page of a general, all-purpose CV. For specific jobs you might need to include your citizenship or what languages you speak. Some people like to include a passport-size photograph on the first page.

2. *Education*

When listing your educational achievements you should always start with your most recent study and work backwards. Include programmes of study that you are presently undertaking and indicate when you will complete the course.

Lay out this section in a way that is easy for the reader to understand. Figure 8.4 gives an example.

EDUCATION	
Tertiary Education	
1992–1995	B.Sci (Plant Biology) Massey University, Palmerston North
1991–1992	Certificate in Greenkeeping Manawatu Polytechnic
Secondary Education	
1986–1990	"A" Bursary Colenso High School, Napier

Figure 8.4:   Education Section of a CV

Note that you only need to state your highest school qualification when detailing your secondary education – unless you are a recent school leaver, in which case you might include details of School Certificate.

You should remember to include in this section any prizes or awards you received.

3. Work Background

In a general, generic CV you would include every job you had ever engaged in. However, when you are applying for a particular job, you would only include relevant work history. For example, if you were applying for a research scientist's position, you would probably not include in your CV the six-week job working at a kindergarten over a summer break or the three-week position as a pool attendant in the mid-semester break last year. But you would include the 12-month position in a Merchant Bank in London when you took a break from study for a year.

There are two approaches to laying out your Work Background section. The first is to write the section in reverse chronological order, as you did in your Educational Background. Or, if you have an extensive work history, you might group your employment experiences into specific areas of work, e.g. research experience and business experience.

4. Personal Strengths

This section is important – but often overlooked or undervalued by CV writers. You are far more than your work experience and education. Are you good at working with groups? Are you a team player? Or do you have the self-discipline and motivation to work alone and meet self-imposed deadlines? How computer literate are you? What software packages are you familiar with? Do you have excellent writing skills or are you an experienced public speaker? Do you have data analysis skills?

All these factors contribute to what you can offer an employer. Lots of people have BScs or degrees in animal science – it is these extra factors that may give you the leading edge. Group your special skills under sub-headings and present them concisely.

5. Interests

In this section you should include any hobbies, community activities, sports and professional interests. If you have taken any leadership roles in these activities then include this information. The fact that you were the President of the local School Board or Model Train Society may seem unimportant but it does suggest that you have leadership experience and decision-making and organisational abilities.

6. *Referees*

Finally, include a short list of referees whom your potential employer may contact. Never list a person as a referee until you have asked them if they are happy to play that role for you. Try to get a balance for your referees – it is a good idea to include someone who can speak for you in an educational environment and someone who can attest to your work abilities.

The layout of your CV is critical and if you are unsure of your ability to format material professionally, get someone else to do it for you. Leave plenty of white space on the page and keep your wording to a minimum. Use a hierarchy of headings to differentiate between material. Your CV (and its covering letter) should differentiate you from the other applicants, so take your time over presentation and get it right!

9. Presenting Data

9.1 Introduction

Using graphics in your reports is an excellent way of focusing your audience's attention on the points you are making and presenting your points in a manner that is easy for your audience to understand. But as graphics are also a great way to confuse or inadvertently mislead your audience, it is important that you know which type of graphic is appropriate to use, when to use it, and how to use it. The rules and points of style that we will introduce you to in this chapter are fairly general and are designed to increase your confidence in what you are doing. If your department, faculty or institute requires you to follow a specific style, then refer to the appropriate style manual.

There are two types of graphics: tables and figures. Tables are best suited to displaying specific, related facts, data or statistics in a small space. You can present data more concisely in tables than you can in text, and more accurately than you can achieve with figures. Detailed comparisons among different groups within the data are often easier to display in a table than in a figure, and nearly always easier to express than in text. On the other hand, figures are an excellent method of displaying trends, general comparisons, movements, distributions and cycles in your data.

Before introducing you to some of the finer points of tables and figures, let's pause to affirm the overarching principle of their use in all forms of writing. Simply stated:

> *Graphics should document or clarify, but not duplicate, data given in text or other graphics.*

This means that you should never present a graph and a table of the same set of data, or give a verbatim description in your text of data that you have also presented in a graphic. Understand, however, that your text and graphics are dependent on each other. A characteristic of good writers is their ability to link the graphics with their text, using their text to highlight, interpret and discuss the information in the graphics. If you remember nothing else in this chapter, remember this point.

9.2   Using Tables

(i)   Informal tables

Books on writing style usually distinguish between two types of tables: *informal* and *formal*. An informal table is a euphemism for a simple list. Informal tables achieve their *raison d'être* through being physically separated from the text by at least one empty line above and below the table and often by additional margin space on both sides of the table. It is this separation which sets informal tables apart from the text and gives them their visual attraction and attention from your audience. Unlike formal tables (as you will soon see), informal tables do not have headings (titles), nor are they numbered. Usually each line of the informal table will be bulleted. For example, if we were to summarise the main characteristics of informal tables in an informal table, we would note that informal tables are:

- separated from the main text by white space
- displayed without any headers or number
- bulleted (although this is an optional extra)
- just simple lists.

(ii)   Formal tables

At first you may not like constructing formal tables because they require more effort to build than simple informal tables. But do persevere in developing this skill, because the value of formal tables for presenting complex information concisely, accurately and clearly more than compensates for the extra effort required in their construction. But before you expend the effort, decide whether or not a formal table is appropriate.

Use the following checklist to decide when a formal table is appropriate:

- you have more than six items of data to present. You can usually express in your text the relationships and meaning inherent in small numbers of data (i.e. less than six items) without having to resort to creating a table.
- there are more than two outcomes in your data. For example, if some student groups 'passed' oral examinations while other groups 'failed', such information is better presented in your text.
- your data actually contain important information. It is pointless, for example, to set up a table to present data which are not statistically significant in their magnitude. Tables are not the place to archive data (no matter how much time you took to collect them!)

The communicative value of a table depends on how well you link it with your text. It is *not* sufficient to just create a table without providing any reference to it in your text. Link your table to your text through an *interpretative translation* of the data in your table. In an interpretative translation, you discuss the highlights and interpret the main points of the table within a wider discussion of what the information in the table means to the topic of your report. Guide your readers through your table, but don't make the common mistake of literally repeating, in words, the content of the table. Vary the approach you make in linking your table to your text. It quickly becomes very tedious for your audience if they repeatedly meet such phrases as 'Table 1 shows that distributed practice resulted in fewer errors than did massed practice'. Instead, use alternative phrases to achieve the link, e.g. 'Distributed practice resulted in fewer errors than massed practice (Table 1)'.

(iii)   Building the table

Setting up a table so that the data are readily comprehensible to your audience is simple as long as you remember a guiding principle of table construction:

> *Organise the data so that the most important elements read down, not across.*

Before explaining this by way of example, let's first refresh your memory of the basic anatomy of a formal table (Fig. 9.1) and how these components are 'fleshed out' (Table 9.1, p. 95):

In Table 9.1, the boxhead contains the headings for the categories in the stub

The *number* of the table and its *title* always appear at the top of the table.	
The *boxhead* contains the column headings	
The *stub* column(s) lists, row by row, the categories for which the information is being presented.	The data being presented appear in columns in the *body* of the table.
Footnotes go in this section	

Figure 9.1:   Five basic skeletal components of a formal table

column and the body of the table. The stub column contains the litter number and level of food intake (1.0, 2.0 kg/day) variables. The body contains the data on the number of thyroid hormone receptors at the two temperatures. Notice how footnotes in the table present points of clarification of the makeup of the data in the table.

Table 9.1: **Number of thyroid hormone receptors in metabolically active tissues of pigs in relation to temperature and food intake**

Litter	Food [a] intake (kg/day)	Temperature	
		10°C	35°C
1	1.0	43 [b]	126
	2.0	120	157
2	1.0	121	246
	2.0	236	470
3	1.0	43	149
	2.0	46	210
4	1.0	18	41
	2.0	32	81

[a]   Barley-based standard feed containing 12.6 MJ disgestible energy/kg
[b]   SE = 15; n = 20

What are the other important features you should note about this table?

• the title is at the top of the table
• the use of lines is constrained
• each row and column title starts with a capital letter
• there is white space in the table – the data are not cramped together
• the data in the columns in the body of the table are equally spaced
• the data in the columns are decimally aligned
• the table 'stands alone'; the reader does not need to refer to the text to understand the data.

Now, let's get back to the issue of table construction. First, look again at Table 9.1. Notice how it is very easy to compare the number of receptors between temperatures for any combination of litter and food intake. In Table 9.2, the information has been

Table 9.2: Number of thyroid hormone receptors in metabolically active tissues of pigs in relation to temperature and food intake

	Temperature	Food [a] intake level	(kg/day)
Litter	°C	1.0	2.0
1	10	43 [b]	120
	35	126	157
2	10	121	236
	35	246	470
3	10	43	46
	35	149	210
4	10	18	32
	35	41	81

[a] Barley-based standard feed containing 12.6 MJ digestible energy/kg
[b] SE = 15; n = 20

rearranged to make it easier to compare receptor numbers at low or high levels of food intake for each litter and temperature combination.

Finally, look at Table 9.3. This table contains the same information as Tables 9.1 and 9.2, but the layout is designed to aid comparison between two levels of food intake for each litter at each temperature. The important point to recognise in each of these examples is that it is easier to compare numbers in adjacent columns than numbers in adjacent rows. This means that you must carefully consider what are the important comparisons that you want to present to your audience.

9.3   Using Figures

Although the term 'figure' can refer to a photograph, flow-chart, map or diagram, we will focus on the most common type of figure, the graph. Quite simply, graphs present numerical data in visual form. Graphs are excellent devices to show trends or important patterns in your data, or to compare the relative responses of different groups (for example, extraction method, plant species) to some factor (for example, temperature, nutrition, light intensity). Remember, however, that if the data themselves are important, then present them in a table; you should not expect your audience to read data off the axes of a graph. The three

Table 9.3: Number of thyroid hormone receptors in metabolically active tissues of pigs in relation to temperature and food intake

Litter	10°C		35°C	
	1.0 kg[a]/day	2.0 kg/day	1.0 kg/day	2.0 kg/day
1	43 [b]	120	126	157
2	121	236	246	470
3	43	46	149	210
4	18	32	41	81

[a]   Barley-based standard feed containing 12.6 MJ digestible energy/kg
[b] $SE = 15; n = 20$

main types of graph you are most likely to use are *line* graphs, *bar* graphs and *pie* graphs.

(i)   Line graphs

You should use a line graph whenever you what to show the changes in the level or response of some variable (e.g. yield, reaction rate) against some form of continuous variable (e.g. time, concentration). Line graphs are particularly useful for comparing the relationship between two or more groups of data (Fig. 9.2).

There are several points to notice in this example of a line graph:

- the vertical (y) and horizontal (x) axes have simple, clear labels
- the axis labels run parallel with the axes
- a simple font type (sans serif; e.g. Helvetica, Arial) is used
- the unit of measurement (i.e. mean number) of the variable plotted on the horizontal axis is clearly presented in the label
- the two data sets (i.e. meaningful words and non-words) are distinguished from each other by the use of different symbols. You could use different coloured lines or different styles of lines (e.g. a solid line and a dashed or dotted line) to achieve the same purpose
- a key for the distinguishing features is included in the graph
- the title appears at the bottom of the graph

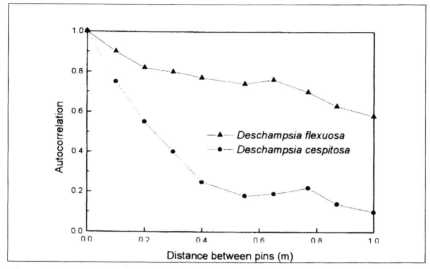

Figure 9.2: Pattern of autocorrelation between scores on pins in frames of point quadrats in relation to distance apart along the frame for two species of *Deschampsia*. Each point is the mean of n=3 replicates

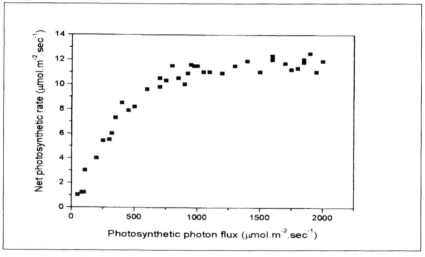

Figure 9.3: Observed net photosynthetic rate (as fixed CO_2) for leaves of *Corylus avellana* cv. Ennis grown in full sun conditions

- as well as the description of the graph, the title contains points of clarification of the data. (Compare this style to that of tables where such information is contained in the footnote section.)

A common version of the line graph is the scattergram (Fig. 9.3). Use scattergrams to illustrate the general relationship between pairs of measured variables. In these graphs, you are trying to show your audience the general pattern of response or relationship between the variables. As a consequence, the points are not joined together.

(ii)   Bar graphs

You will find bar graphs very useful for presenting categorical data (i.e. data measured from separate groups of 'things' such as groups of plants or animals, brands of goods, or type of treatment). Bar graphs share many style character-istics of line graphs: their vertical and horizontal axes are simply and clearly labelled; the units of measure are presented; and the title appears below the figure (Fig. 9.4).

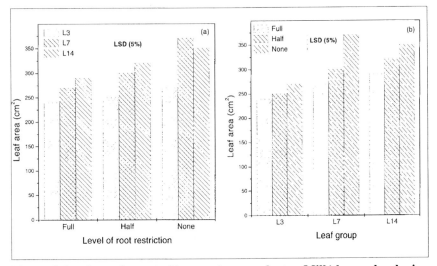

Figure 9.4:   Area of tomato (*Lycopersicon esculentum* Mill.) leaves developing 3 (L3), 7 (L7) and 14 (L14) days after start of physical restriction to all (Full), half (Half), or none (None) of the root system

When you use bar graphs for this purpose, take time to identify the categories important to your comparison. For example, in Figure 9.4(a) the major category is 'level of root restriction' and the minor category is 'leaf group'; these roles are reversed in Figure 9.4(b). Notice the major change in the appearance of the graphs, even though the same data set is being used.

(iii) Pie graphs

Whenever you need to compare percentages of a single whole, then a pie graph (or pie chart) is the graph to use (Fig. 9.5). Provided that you do not have too many wedges (i.e. categories), pie graphs are easy to interpret and have a strong visual impact.

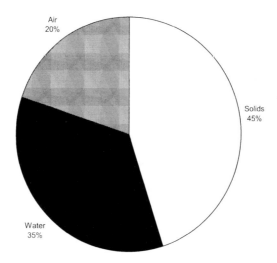

Figure 9.5: 'Ideal' proportion of solids, air, and water for 'excellent' plant growth

The rules of style associated with these graphs are as simple as the graphs themselves:

- make the relative percentages clear by starting at the 12 o'clock position and sequence the wedges clockwise
- sequence the wedges from largest to smallest (although sometimes this is not possible because it is difficult to clearly present the labels of small wedges adjacent to each other)
- give the percentage value of each wedge, either inside each wedge or as part of the label

- keep all the labels horizontal.

Pie graphs are less effective when comparing wholes; in such cases, use a 100 per cent stacked bar (or column) graph.

9.4   Graphics Abuse

Just as words can cloud meaning or mislead, so too can graphs. Try to avoid the following common errors when using graphics.

- Many graphics packages (particularly those associated with spreadsheet packages) offer you *line* and *X-Y* graphs. Line graphs differ from X-Y graphs in the way in which the levels of the variable on the horizontal axis are displayed. In line graphs, the levels are always equally spaced, regardless of their magnitude; in X-Y graphs, the spacing accurately reflects the magnitude of the level. Thus, if your horizontal axis is time (e.g. 1, 2, 5, 12 and 13 weeks), these will appear at equal spacing (incorrect) on a line graph and arithmetically spaced (correct) on an X-Y graph.

- Keep your graphs as simple and uncluttered as possible. Many (spreadsheet) graphics packages, by default, produce grid lines at each major point on the vertical and horizontal axes. Such lines should be 'turned off' because they generally clutter up the graph, distracting your audience from its important information. Similarly, do not be seduced by the wide range of fancy variations of the basic types of graphs that are available in many graphics packages. For example, unless 3D bars actually improve the message of your bar graph, then do not use them (even if they are the default setting!)

- The default (and often the only) position for the title of the graph in many (spreadsheet) graphics packages is at the top of the graph. This position is not acceptable style for the reports you will write. Consequently, you will have to use your wordprocessing program to produce the title and description of your graphs in the correct position – below the graph!

- Many programs allow you to print (wrap) text around one or both sides of your tables and figures. Just because the software allows this does not mean that this is an appropriate style. And for most, if not all, of the reports that you will prepare for your courses, wrapping text around tables and figures is not appropriate style.

- Be honest with your figures, particularly if you are presenting data for which an estimate of the variability (e.g. standard error) is not available or appropriate. We all know that 'a picture is worth a thousand words', but don't forget that 'a picture can hide a hundred "truths".' Look at Figure 9.6a, which plots the yield of tomatoes grown in different proprietary brands of soil-less growing media. It appears as though there are considerable differences in performance between the different brands. Now look at Figure 9.6b. This graph shows the same set of data but against a different scale on the vertical axis. The differences among the brands now appear marginal. Which figure do you think gives a clearer picture of the results?

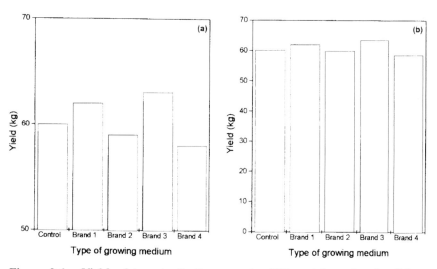

Figure 9.6: **Yield of tomato fruit grown in different brands of soil-less growing media**

9.5 Remember!

A final word about graphics (and yes, we have already mentioned this point, but it is important!). Remember that your audience deserves some guidance with your tables and figures. Do not follow the bad habit of many novice writers who lead their audience to a table or figure with a phrase such as 'The influence of the photosynthetic photon flux levels on photosynthetic rate is shown in Figure 2', and then move onto the next point. Don't leave your audience hanging on your graphics; guide them into the data. Tell your audience what you think the data have revealed. Remember that you are writing a report, not a crossword; your aim is to give a clear description, not to drop clues.

10. Preparing for and Presenting Seminars

10.1 Introduction

At some time most students and professionals are required to speak to an audience. This may be the presentation of a scientific paper; a technical report; advice to clients – there are many possibilities.

Seminars give students the opportunity to present information to an audience, but importantly, also provide the opportunity for feedback. Seminars are not lecture presentations – they are designed to generate questions and discussion.

To some people, speaking in public comes relatively easily, while for others, having to face an audience is a truly nerve-racking experience. However, even the most experienced public speakers are often anxious, keyed-up and nervous before they begin speaking. This is a normal human reaction ("stage fright" is a severe form), the fear usually being a result of your desire to do well, to have a rapport with the audience.

To overcome this nervousness, the experienced speaker:

- is thoroughly prepared
- is positive
- knows the audience (who are they? what are their needs?)
- talks confidently and enthusiastically
- speaks slowly (uses short sentences)
- uses eye contact
- uses pauses
- uses aids (slides, acetates, etc.) purposefully
- concludes firmly and confidently
- PRACTISES.

This guide offers a few suggestions which may assist you. There is no single correct way to give a seminar, each person has their own individual style. Nevertheless, there are a few general rules which you should consider carefully before deciding to break them and a few pitfalls to avoid at all costs. Hopefully the ideas here will help you to make a clearer presentation, keep the audience interested and perhaps even encourage you to enjoy yourself!

10.2 Planning

This stage is the key. There are one or two people in every hundred who can talk for 30–40 minutes about a topic in an organised, understandable way at a moment's notice. Another 10 or so have the confidence to try, but should never have done so. Most of us need to prepare very carefully.

Seminars must have a beginning, a middle and an end. Very obvious? It is amazing how many seminars are given where the presenter plunges straight into the body of the seminar without warning, or suddenly stops without presenting any general discussion or conclusion.

1. *The Introduction*

This should clearly set out the scope and importance of the topic. It should:

- explain why it is an issue or a problem and why it is important.
- briefly summarise any necessary background (context) information, historical details, specialist terminology, etc.
- give the audience an idea of what you intend to discuss with a **clear statement of the objectives or the aspects of the study you intend covering in the presentation**.

2. *The Body of the Seminar*

Here the essentials of your topic are presented along with the information/results you obtained. Your findings/arguments are then discussed.

- focus clearly on your topic.
- do not present information you don't intend to discuss.
- build up your story slowly and logically.
- recap if the story becomes a complicated one.
- aim to keep the audience with you.

3. *Conclusions*

Finally, discuss the implications of the information you have presented, your own ideas and what you think it all means.

10.3   Preparation

Having planned what you are going to say, spend some time considering how you are going to present it. What visual aids are you going to use? Plan them with the audience in mind, remembering that most of them will not have had any experience of your topic. If you do this carefully, visual aids can make the seminar much easier for the audience to follow **and** much easier for you to present.

Most people will use either Powerpoint or overhead projection (OHP) sheets. There are some clear guidelines here:

- use a legible, large font. The font size should be at least 15 points, possibly much larger
- create a professional template
- *look* at the slide when it goes up on the screen. Check the audience can see what you want it to see.
- *explain* the details of your figure or table.
- pause and give people time to look at your overhead.
- check how to work the equipment before the seminar!
- do not block the screen by standing in the line of vision.
- do not put too much information on one slide.
- do not include unnecessary information.
- summarise the main point(s) of each overhead as you show it.
- don't distract with too many graphics or fancy techniques: keep slides clear and understandable.

Remember: Each slide you show should have a purpose, and you should help the audience recognise what that purpose is.

10.4   Types of Delivery

There are four possible ways to deliver a presentation.

- Manuscript method   = read directly from prepared text; not recommended for a seminar presentation because it becomes monotonous and there is no contact with the audience who will quickly become inattentive.
- Memory method   = memorise the entire presentation; not recommended for a seminar presentation because of the danger of memory loss!
- Impromptu method   = no preparation, make it up as you go along; not recommended for a seminar presentation because

you are wasting everyone's time!

- Extemporaneous method = using an outline, or key phrases or brief notes; recommended for a seminar presentation because it has the advantages of good eye contact, naturalness of language, rhythm, pace and voice modulation.

10.5   Timing a Seminar

Planning your seminar so it does not go on too long can often be a problem. Experience can be a guide, but if you do not have much experience, careful rehearsal is the only answer. Remember that in a rehearsal it is very easy to go much faster than you should in front of an audience. Make sure you are clear about how much time you have available for your actual presentation, and how much you are expected to leave for questions and discussion.

You may find it useful to put check timings on your notes to make sure you are not over-running too much.

Do not keep to time by speeding up your presentation
Do not keep to time by leaving out your conclusion

As a safeguard, it is often a good idea to have some optional material prepared which can be left out if, on the day, you find that you are over-running. If you find yourself in this situation make sure you leave the optional item out completely – do not skip through it very quickly and confuse your audience.

10.6   Pause, Poise and Presence of Mind

Remember that pauses during visual aids help your audience – they get time to assimilate and understand what you are saying. Try to keep an eye on the audience and check that they appear to be following you. Pay particular attention to those who looked enthusiastic and interested at the start. Reference to these people will give you confidence if they continue to look interested as the seminar progresses.

Pauses can help you too. They can help you relax, collect your thoughts and think carefully about what you are going to say next.

Apart from this, confidence comes from the knowledge that you have prepared as best you can and that you know and understand your material well.

10.7   Handling Questions at the End of the Seminar

- Listen carefully.
- If you do not understand the question, don't guess. Ask the questioner to repeat

what he or she said.

- If you still do not understand, ask the seminar chairperson for help.
- If you have no idea of the answer, say so immediately! Do not waffle.
- There is no substitute for good preparation and good understanding of your topic.

10.8 Summary and Helpful Hints

1. *Before Your Seminar*

- Practise beforehand (days if possible) – practice does make perfect!
- Make sure you can pronounce all the words.
- Make sure you are thoroughly prepared, and that any aids (the projector, for example) are working. Ensure slides can be seen from the back of the room, and that you can use them effectively.
- Look your best – looking good helps you feel good, which helps your confidence.
- Be aware of your distracting mannerisms (e.g. pen clicking, saying "ah" or "um" every 15 seconds). What can you do to control them?
- Keep jargon and technical words to an absolute minimum.
- Anticipate questions – think of some answers beforehand if possible.

2. *During your Presentation*

- Communicate first – keep your mind on your message.
- Keep to the point – do not waffle.
- Speak clearly but not too slowly.
- Talk to everyone in your audience (not the floor or a spot on the back wall); make eye contact.
- Use open gestures; try to look relaxed; do not pace up and down.
- If you think a pause is required, use silence, not "ums" and "ahs".
- Keep to time.

Directive for lulling an audience to sleep

Wear a dark suit and conventional tie; turn down the lights;
close the curtains; display a crowded slide and leave
it in place; stand still; *read* your paper without looking up;
read steadily with no marked changes in cadence; show no
pictures; use grandiloquent words and long sentences.

(Booth, 1993)

11. Using Secondary Material

One of the features of scientific writing is the requirement that you place your argument or analysis within a scholarly context; that is, that you cite the ideas of other authors. Incorporating the ideas of other writers into your work is a skill you need to learn for all aspects of postgraduate writing if you are to achieve a satisfactory outcome.

11.1   Terminology

First of all, let's look at some terms which relate to using sources in your writing.

1.   Academic or secondary source

An academic source (or a secondary source) refers to any piece of material that you use when you are writing on a particular topic. This may include an article in a journal, an article in the *Listener*, a book or a radio interview – anything that influences your discussion of a particular topic.

2.   Quoting

A quotation is an exact copy of a passage from another source – it is a word-for-word transcript of someone else's words. Although rarely used in scientific writing, if you use a quotation, you must indicate on your script that this is a quotation (by indenting the passage or putting it in quotation marks) and you must reference it correctly (for more detail on this, *see* Chapter 12).

3.   Citing

Citing involves using someone else's ideas or data but expressing those ideas in your own words. For example, here is a quotation from Minichiello et al.'s text: *In-depth interviewing: Researching people*:

> In-depth interviewing when used in social science research gives access
> to knowledge – a knowledge of meanings and interpretations that
> individuals give to their lives and events (p. 1).

The text referred to above is one of the many books you have read on the subject. You want to include the ideas contained in the text but, to present them fluently, you choose to use your own words, i.e. you choose to *cite* Minichiello *et al*. Here is one way you might do this:

> Minichiello *et al.* (1990) present perhaps the most straightforward description of the purpose of in-depth interviews in qualitative research. They suggest that in-depth interviews in the context of social science research (and this might include systems research) indicate how people view their personal experience.

Note that when you cite information, you still need to acknowledge the source. Again, refer to Chapter 12 for more detail on how to reference citations.

4.   Plagiarism

Plagiarism involves representing someone else's ideas, research or text, as your own. It is a form of stealing and, as such, is treated very seriously by most tertiary organisations. Learn to use the correct referencing conventions and be scrupulous about acknowledging sources. Never copy from another person's work or text (this includes the Internet).

11.2   When to Reference Citations

Referencing citations can cause problems for students: how do you decide what should be referenced? What if you are dealing with a very common and widely known issue? For example, you read in a book that 'without investment in research and development, New Zealand cannot continue to grow' and you want to express this idea in your assignment. But surely it is such a widely held view that it doesn't warrant referencing? Should you reference this idea?

If you are writing a report for a particular audience (for example, the Head of a CRI), you can answer this question simply: if the person you are writing for is likely to be generally familiar with the idea, then you probably don't need to reference it.

However, an assignment is more difficult to assess because your audience is not so clearly defined. Perhaps an analogy would help.

Imagine you are playing for a club cricket (or netball) team and you are discussing strategies for an upcoming game with team-mates. Everyone in the group will know certain things: what the rules of the game are, what the names of the positions are, whether you are playing home or away. In the same way, when you are writing in a particular discipline, certain pieces of knowledge are shared information. These do not need to be documented for the same reason that you do not take the time to explain to your team-mates what a wicket keeper (or goal keep) is.

However, in your meeting, some things will be known only to one person. The captain may have played the opposing team before and remembers a weak player;

another player may remember that the pitch tends to be slow, even in mid-summer. These ideas are expressed by single voices; they are not shared knowledge and so should be attributed to particular sources.

Documenting an assignment works in the same way. For example, it is common knowledge amongst people working in the sciences and applied sciences that funding approaches to research have changed in New Zealand over the last 15 years. So, if you were writing an assignment which included this piece of information, you would probably not need to find a reference to support your statement. But if you find an author who does discuss specific ways in which approaches to funding and levels of funding have changed, or someone who provides numerical data on the subject, then you would reference that source in your assignment.

Once you become familiar with a subject area, you will develop a sense of what needs to be referenced. But, if you are in any doubt, provide a reference; you are unlikely to be penalised for providing too many.

11.3   How to Use Sources

The next skill to develop is a judgement of *how* to use other authors in your work. Reports and assignments use secondary sources quite differently.

1.   Assignments

A problem commonly raised by students is 'does my lecturer or supervisor want to know what *I* think, or do they just want to hear what everyone else has said?' It is an interesting question, and not easily answered (try asking one of your lecturers sometime).

Your lecturer, generally, does want to know what *you* think. But they want to know what you think *in the context of the scholarly debate on the topic*. In other words, they want to hear *you* play the solo instrument, but with the whole orchestra supporting you in the background.

An important point to realise is that there is an academic debate on every scholarly subject. Your marker wants you to position yourself within that debate. So, your assignment should define the parameters and the points in between *and where you stand in the debate* (and why).

Let's use an example. You are writing an assignment on the following topic:

> 'Agriculture remains – and will continue to remain in the foreseeable
> future – the cornerstone of our national economy.'

Now, as you read other writers on the topic, you may find some that think agriculture has indeed remained and will continue to remain the cornerstone of our economy. Others say that agriculture has had its day and other industry is developing as the forefront of our economy. Yet others discuss the way in which agriculture has had to change to stay ahead of the market and how, if such intelligent strategic decisions continue to be made, agriculture may be able to continue as the cornerstone of our economy. Weighing up the evidence, you may wish to adopt a position close to the latter view: yes, agriculture is still there at the base of our economy and is showing a capacity to change and to stay in this pivotal position, but unless it is able to maintain the impetus of change and strategic understanding of the market, it could become subsumed under other industry leaders.

The whole thrust of your assignment, then, should be to explain and defend *your* position. But you should also explain who is on the perimeters of the debate and what the other positions are. If you have allied yourself with another writer, explain why you find their evidence so compelling and the others' perspective limited.

To go back to our orchestral image: your proposition (and the defence of that proposition) is your solo; the orchestra is composed of the ideas of others, and all these parts, solo and orchestral, are vital to the work as a whole.

2. *Reports*

Because the purpose of a report is invariably *practical* (i.e. what should be done in a certain situation), you use the ideas of other authors to support your own practical observations. For example,

> The organisation has grown so rapidly that its strategic plan (which was always vague and non-specific) is now almost totally irrelevant and inapplicable. Thus the institution lacks direction; as Gilbert *et al.* (2002) observe, a bad plan will cause the organisation to suffer.

Academic sources are used in the discussion section of your report to back up your practical analysis and solutions. They show the reader that you have some credibility, some authority and weight behind your statements. In the above example you are showing that you are not alone in thinking that poor planning can cause problems – other authorities have noted poor planning as a problem for other organisations.

11.4 Integration

Finally, a word about incorporating the ideas of others into your work. Remember that any assignment you write should be an integrated whole. Quotations (when used) and citations should be worked into your assignment so that they become an integral part of it.

While it is rare to use quotations in scientific writing, if you do decide to use one, never leave a quotation to stand alone or speak for itself. Introduce a quotation by letting the reader know your opinion of it: do you agree or disagree? Or do you feel that the author is only partially correct? Why? What are the limitations of this idea? How does this idea compare with someone else's? After the quotation, comment further or develop the idea in some way.

As your experience in writing scientific assignments grows, and as your knowledge of the subject you are studying develops, you will find that incorporating the ideas of others fluently and elegantly into your own work becomes easier. Like all aspects of writing, this is a skill which develops with practice.

12. Referencing APA Style

Referencing is an important part of all academic work. Sources of information should be acknowledged for the following reasons:

- to distinguish between your ideas and someone else's.
- to show readers the range and quality of your reading.
- to direct readers to the sources used, if they want further information.

Failure to acknowledge a source of information, or using other people's ideas as your own, is called **plagiarism**, and is a serious form of academic dishonesty.

While there are many different sets of conventions for referencing – and if you ever publish research you will find that many journals have their own in-house style – many science faculties use the formatting conventions of the American Psychological Association for setting out references. Some of these conventions are listed below. For more detail on APA referencing you should refer to the *Publication Manual of the American Psychological Association* (5th ed.).

12.1   Acknowledging Sources

The APA style of referencing uses in-line acknowledgement of sources rather than footnotes or endnotes. This means that sources need to be acknowledged in the ways listed below.

1. How Do I Acknowledge an Idea which I have Expressed in My Own Words?

Sometimes someone else's ideas, concepts or figures, but not that person's exact words may be included in your work. This is called **citing** or **paraphrasing** (as opposed to quoting, when you use someone's exact words). In this situation, the source must be acknowledged by putting the author's last name and the date when the work was published in brackets at the end of the sentence.

> Management consultants usually see the formulation of a strategic plan as an essential step for all organisations (McKendrey, 2002).
>
> Many entrepreneurs see educational qualifications as irrelevant (Fergusson, 2001; McKendrey, 2002).

Note that in the second example above, where two sources are cited, each one is separated with a semicolon.

Another approach to this is to include the surname of the author within your sentence with the date in brackets, like this:

> As McKendrey (2002) suggests, entrepreneurs see educational qualifications as irrelevant.

2. How Do I Include a Short Quotation in My Work?

If the author's own words are being used, put the quotation in quotation marks and include a page number at the end of the reference.

> For many New Zealanders, this country is no longer an agricultural nation. New Zealand has grown, diversified and bounced back again, determined never again to be reliant on a single industry and market. "We have come of age, internationally" (Anderson, 2002, p. 64).

NB   When the quotation ends a sentence, the full stop comes **after** the information in brackets.

3. How Do I Include a Longer Quotation in My Work?

If a direct quotation which is longer than either two sentences or 20 words is being used, the quotation should be indented five spaces and quotation marks **omitted**. The reference should be acknowledged in the same way as the shorter quotation above.

> Within management theory there have been many changes and developments. One researcher – Sharryn Williams – has identified a key factor for management sources: communication.
>
>> Communication is a vital factor in determining managerial success. A successful manager establishes links throughout her organisation, formal and informal, upwards, downwards and horizontally. Two vital measures of success are these: a respect for formal procedures and a recognition of the value of the informal network (2003, p. 6).
>
> Such a perspective has support from many other theorists in the area...

4. How Do I Reference an Author who is Quoted in a Book/Journal I am Reading?

If you wish to use a quotation or cite an idea which is quoted or cited by another author, then both sources should be acknowledged in the text as follows:

> Although much has been written about the negative impact of stress, "nevertheless, stress can contribute to performance" (Ward, 1998, p. 33 cited in Bowling, 2001, p. 16).
>
> Although many authors have emphasised the way in which stress can impact negatively on performance, Ward (1998, cited in Bowling, 2001) emphasises its positive aspects.

The Reference list, at the end of the assignment, would list only Bowling, **not** Ward.

5. How Do I Reference a Source if I have Already Used the Author's Name in the Sentence?

Sometimes an author may be directly referred to within the assignment.

> - Magnall (1994) was the first to maintain that ...
> - Planning is the first essential step according to Magnall (1994).
> - Researchers in the field (Magnall, 1994; Crews, 2002) indicate that ...
> - He stated that "the management cycle has four key elements" (Magnall, 1994, p. 16) but did not rank those four factors.

6. How Do I Reference Two Works by the Same Author?

If referring to two or more works by the same author, both published in the same year, the first has an "a" after the date, the second has a "b" and so on:

> In her next study of the problem (Lenart, 2001b), she considered other factors.

The author's name would then appear twice (or more often) in the references section at the end of the paper, with the appropriate small letter beside the date.

7. How Do I Reference a Work with Many Authors?

If a work has three or more authors, all names should be listed in the first citation, but *et al.* (meaning "and others") may be used in subsequent citations:

First citation	Coles, Emerson & Ormsby (1992) found that ...
Subsequent citations	Coles *et al* (1992) also found ...

8. How Do I Reference a Letter, Email or Interview?

Anything that isn't accessible to other people (i.e. not published in any way) is called a **personal communication**. It is not included in the reference list but should be cited in the text. Give initials of the communicator and an exact date.

E. C. MacKay, personal communication, December 9 , 2001

9. How Do I Reference Something with No Author, Such as Some Newspaper Articles or Legal Material?

If you are referring to something that has no acknowledged author, then substitute the first few words of the title in double quotation marks.

"Dollar plummets", 2004

Most legal material is cited in text in this way, but details of how specific types of legal material should be formatted in the text may be found in Appendix D of the *APA Style Manual* (5th Edition) or visit http://www.lib.wsc.ma.edu/legalapa.htm.

10. How do I Cite an Electronic Source (e.g. a web page) in the Body of an Argument?

A web page or website is acknowledged in the text in the same way as other texts, i.e. you state the author (or corporate author), year of publication, and a page number for a direct quote. If no page numbers are indicated in the source, give paragraph number e.g. (McKenzie, 2004, para 14).

More ephemeral forms of electronic sources, e.g. email, forum discussion etc, should be referenced as personal communications.

12.2　What is a Reference List?

A reference list is a list of the full bibliographical details of all the material quoted or cited in your assignment. Every assignment written must have a reference list. It should be started on a new page and be headed "References".

In listing the references at the end of the document, one style guide should be followed consistently. We recommend that you use the following format, taken from the *Publication manual of the American Psychological Association (APA)* (5th ed.).

All items must be listed in alphabetical order, according to the surname of the first author.

1. How Do I List a Book According to APA Style?

Put the author's surname first, spelled out in full, with initials only for first and second names. Give the date of publication in brackets. Next comes the *title*, city of publication and publisher. Note that on the reference page only the first letter of the first word of the title and subtitle is capitalised. Title and subtitle should be underlined or italicised. Either is acceptable. The title is followed by a full stop. A colon (:) separates the place of publication from the publisher's name.

The following list gives examples of the most commonly used types of referencing using this referencing style.

a. *Single Author*
   Sligo, F. (1991). *Organisational behaviour: Case studies and commentaries.* Palmerston North: Dunmore Press.

b. *Single Author, later edition*
   May, C. (1992). *Effective writing: A handbook for accountants* (3rd ed.). Englewood Cliffs, New Jersey: Prentice-Hall, Inc.

c. *Two Authors*
   Strunk, W., Jr., & White, E.B. (1979). *The elements of style* (3rd ed.). New York: Macmillan.

d. *Corporate Author*
   American Psychological Association. (2004). *Publication manual of the American*

Psychological Association. (5th ed.). Washington, DC: Author.

e. *Edited Book*

Jackson, R., & Buckland, T. (Eds.). (1992). *Summer schools: A unique grouping.* London: Oxford University Press.

f. *Article or Chapter in Edited Book*

Mellallieu, P. J. (1993). The postmodernist manager. In P. J. Mellallieu & N. Boneparte (Eds.), *The manager: Missionary, magician and megalomaniac* (pp. 134–159). New York: John Wiley and Sons.

2. *How Do I Reference a Periodical?*

Periodicals are anything that is published on a regular basis – magazines, journals and newspapers. Sometimes it is difficult to distinguish between journals and magazines, but here is a general rule of thumb: if the articles in the periodical have a reference section (i.e. if they list their sources in some academically conventional way) then it can be regarded as a journal; if they do not have a reference section, then treat it as a magazine.

Periodicals are referenced as follows:

Titles of periodicals should be quoted in full and italicised (or underlined) and followed by volume numbers, italicised, and page numbers, not italicised. Titles of articles should not be italicised, underlined or placed in inverted commas.

a. *Journal Article, One Author*

Ferguson, I. S. (2003). Forecasting the future for timber. *The Australian Journal of Agricultural Economics, 18,* 562–578.

b. *Journal Article, Two Authors, Journal Paginated by Issue*

Becker, L.J., & Seligman, C. (2001). Welcome to the energy crisis. *Journal of Social Issues, 37,* 2, 1–7.

Note that: if the journal is paginated by volume rather than issue, then you do not include the issue number.

c. *Magazine Article*

Emerson, A.M. (2004, December 10–17). Bald is beautiful. *The Listener,* 16.

d. *Newspaper Article, No Author*
Students attack Todd report. (2004, June 16). *The Dominion*, 3.

e. *Newspaper Article, Author Known*
Robinson, L. (2004, July 19). The new orthodoxy. *The Dominion*, 9.

f. *Newsletter Article, Corporate Author*
Staff (2002, September 3). Why students should pay more. *National Business Review*, 7.

3. *How Do I Reference Internet Sources?*

a. *Web Page*
O'Connor, R.E. (2004). *Managing music*. Retrieved August 19, 2004 from http://www.musicresourcesNZ/management.asp.

b. *Online Periodical*
Hills, S.J. (2003). Soaring above: Managing educational change. *Education Resource Management in Aoteaora/New Zealand, 16*, 443-449. Retrieved March 24, 2003 from http://www.EdResource.massey.ac.nz/management/focus.asp.

Note re author: if the web page does not have a specified author, see if you can find a corporate author. If neither is available, move the title into the author's position.

Note re access details: always provide the full URL and the exact date of retrieval. Since materials on the Internet can change very quickly, you must be exact about the timing and location of your source material.

Note re date: if no date is available, put n.d. in the date position.

4. *How Do I Reference Technical Research Reports?*

Hewitt, A. (1999). *Sexual stereotyping in advertisements for children* (Report No. 634–3964). Washington DC: International Marketing Association.

5. *How Do I Reference Unpublished Theses?*

Knowles, G. A. (2001). *New methods for old*. Unpublished doctoral dissertation, Massey University, Palmerston North, New Zealand.

Frawley, E. A. (2002). *Nobody does it better; English sheep farmers face the world*. Unpublished master's thesis, Sussex University, Brighton.

6. *How Do I Reference Annual Reports?*

Annual reports are referenced as books with corporate authors (see above).

7. *How Do I Reference Study Guide Material?*

If you cite articles or excerpts from books which are reprinted in Study Guides, refer to the article or book directly (your Study Guide **should** contain full bibliographical information!)

If the material being cited is not part of a reprinted article or book, it should be referenced as follows:

a. Where the Study Guide has an Identified Author:
Emerson, J. M. (2004). *Teaching the gifted child: Study guide 2*. Palmerston North: College of Education, Massey University.

b. Where the Study Guide has No Identified Author:
Department of Management Systems, College of Business. (2004). *26.120 Introduction to organisation and management*. Palmerston North: Massey University.

8. *How Do I Reference Abstracts from a Database or From a List of Abstracts?*

James, F., & Burrow, G.M. (2002). The pessimistic manager meets the marketing manager. *Journal of Multi-Strategic Development, 19*, 417-420. Abstract retrieved November 19, 2004, from ERIC database.

9. *How Do I Cite Computer Programmes?*

Picard, J. L. (1995). Captain's log: Metacognitive modelling (Version 5.0) [Computer Software]. Paris: Enterprise Software Services, Inc.

10. *How Do I Cite a Personal Communication?*

Sometimes you will need to acknowledge personal communication as a source of information. This includes lecture notes, memos, e-mail messages, interviews and the like. Personal communication is NOT included in a reference list or bibliography – you should only cite personal communications in the text of your assignment.

11. Where Do I Find Information about Referencing Materials not Mentioned Here?

For details on how to format other, more unusual material, (e.g. proceedings of meetings and symposia, films, TV programmes, individual interviews) refer to the *Publication manual of the American Psychological Association*, Edition 5, also referred to as the APA Style Manual. Another useful source of information is http://owl.english.purdue.edu/handouts/research/r_apa.html

12. What is a Bibliography?

As mentioned above, a reference list should contain **only** the material you have cited in your text. If other material as background reading has been used it may be included in a new list called the **Bibliography**. Format material in exactly the same way as in the reference section.

13(a) References

There are many useful books available to help you improve your writing. Search the writing section of the Massey Library (808) or, if you are an extramural student, your local library, to find books that seem helpful.

The list that follows gives details of books and manuals used in the writing of these Writing Guidelines. All would give further helpful directions on writing issues.

Ary, D., Jacobs, & L.C.; Razevieh, A. (Ed.) (1979). *Introduction to research in education.* New York, Holt: Rinehart and Winston.

Booth, V. (1993). *Communicating in science.* (2nd ed.) Cambridge: Cambridge University Press.

Brennan, M.C. (1990). *Style handbook: Department of Marketing.* Palmerston North, Business Studies Faculty: Massey University.

Day, R.A. (1989). *How to write and publish a scientific paper.* (3rd ed.) Cambridge: Cambridge University Press.

Day, R.A. (1992). *Scientific English – a guide for scientists and other professionals.* Phoenix: Orynx Press.

Elder, B. (1994). *Communication skills.* Melbourne: Macmillan Education, Australia Pty Ltd.

Montagnes, I. (1991). *Editing and publication: a training manual.* Manila, International Rice Research Institute: Ottawa, International Development Research Centre.

Van Emden, J. (2001). *Effective Communication for Science Teachers.* London, UK: Palgrave

Penrose, A.M., & Katz, S.B. (2004). *Writing in the Sciences.* (2nd ed.) New York: Pearson Longman.

Purdue University (2004). *Online Writing Laboratory.*Retrieved from http://owl.english.purdue.edu/handouts/research/r_apa.html

13(b) Bibliography

Adamson, G., & Prentice, J. (1987). *Communication skills in practice 1. Speaking and listening*. Melbourne: Nelson Wadsworth.

Bate, D., & Sharpe, P. (1990). *Student writer's handbook*. London: Harcourt & Brace Jovanovich Inc.

Booher, D. (1983). *Would you put that in writing?* New York: Facts on File Inc.

Clancy, J., & Ballard, B. (1981). *Essay writing for students*. Melbourne: Longman Cheshire.

Crystal, D. (1988). *Rediscover grammar*. Essex: Longmans.

Emerson, L. (Ed.) (2000). *Assignment writing guidelines for business students* (2nd ed.). Palmerston North: Dunmore Press.

Flower, L. (1985). *Problem solving strategies for writing* (2nd ed.). New York: Harcourt Brace Jovanovich.

Gilbert, M.B. (1983). *Clear writing: A business guide*. New York: John Wiley & Sons Inc.

Lobban, C.S., & Schefter, M. (1992). *Successful lab reports*. Cambridge: CUP.

Michaelson, H.B. (1990). *How to write and publish engineering papers and reports*. Phoenix: Oryx Press.

New Zealand Government Printing Office (1981). *Style book* (3rd ed.). Wellington: Government Printer.

O'Connor, M. (1991). *Writing successfully in science*. London: Chapman and Hall.

Sides, C.H. (1992). *How to write and present technical information* (2nd ed.). Cambridge: Cambridge University Press.

Sligo, F. (1994). *Effective communication in business* (2nd ed.). Palmerston North: Software Technology Ltd.

Strunk, W. Jr., & White, E.B. (1979). *The elements of style* (3rd ed.). New York: MacMillan Co.

Trimble, L. (1985). *English for science and technology*. London: CUP.

Turk, C., & Kirkman, J. (1982). *Effective writing: Improving scientific technical and business communications*. London: E. & F.N. Spon.

Venolia, J. (1987). *Rewrite right!* Berkeley, California: Ten Speed Press.

Watkins, F.C., & Dillingham, W.B. (1986). *Practical English handbook* (7th ed.). Boston: Houghton Mifflin Co.

Appendix A
Presentation of Documents

1.   Introduction

The presentation of a piece of writing is important. A well prepared document looks professional and credible. Clear presentation can prevent misinterpretation of content and should help the reader understand the material.

The following information should be considered a *guide* to presentation, rather than directives. Be flexible. Consider the needs of the reader and the format of a particular piece of writing when deciding on an appropriate presentation.

2.   Page Numbering

Each page, except the title page, should be numbered at the centre of the bottom of the page. Pages preceding the body of a report (e.g. Executive Summary, Table of Contents) are numbered in lower case Roman numerals. In the body of all assignments, the pages are numbered in Arabic numerals.

3.   Line Spacing

Assignments should be double-spaced so that there is room for the marker's comments. Reports and theses are usually 1.5 spacing.

For reports, each major section should begin on a new page.

4.   Headings and Numbering

Where headings are appropriate, major section headings should be capitalised and, where appropriate, numbered 1, 2, 3, etc. Subheadings with each section should be upper/lower case (for example as in Fig. A.1), and numbered 1.1, 1.2, etc. An assignment should require no more than two levels of numbered headings (1.4.3.7 is difficult for the reader to understand within the context of the structure of your work), although a thesis may require more. If subsections are needed, do not number the minor headings.

All headings should be printed in bold and begin at the left margin. Headings at the top level should be in capitals; only the first letter of each major word should be capitalised for headings at lower levels (Fig. A.1).

```
1.      INTRODUCTION

1.1     Background of the company

        History

        Management structure

2.      DISCUSSION

2.1     Breakdown of Authority

        Senior management

        Supervisors


                    2
```

Figure A.1:   Levels and presentation of headings

Remember, presentation is an important aid to the reader's understanding and also helps establish your own professionalism.

5.   Paragraphs

Do not indent the first line. The text should be flush with the left margin and right-justified. It should begin two blank lines under top level or second-level headings, and one line under lower-level headings. Leave a single blank line between paragraphs.

6.   Quotations in the Text

See Chapter 12, Referencing.

7.   Acronyms

Acronyms are used to abbreviate long titles or clumsy expressions. Examples include NZ for New Zealand and CEO for Chief Executive Officer.

Acronyms are acceptable as long as they do not detract from the reader's easy need to continually check meanings which may affect their understanding of and response to your text. For this reason, use acronyms cautiously.

The first time an acronym is presented it should be written out in full and the acronym should be placed in brackets immediately afterwards. From then on the acronym can be used without further explanation.

e.g. Most Crown Research Institutes (CRIs) were required to change their funding strategies.

Print acronyms without spaces or stops. For example:

USA	not	U S A	or	U.S.A.
SUWAC	not	S U W A C	or	S.U.W.A.C.

8.   Numbers

The general rule is to use words to express numbers below 10 and numerals to express numbers 10 and above. However, numbers coming at the beginning of a sentence should be expressed as words.

e.g. Twelve officers remained on the scene and four of these were to remain there throughout the night. The next day, reinforcements of 24 men were brought in, 12 of whom combed the adjacent area.

Appendix B:
English and Science

1. Introduction

With the many and varied topics which you will encounter in Applied Science, you will contend with some extremely complicated problems. It is therefore important to use language which provides precise descriptions of these complex problems and concepts. We are fortunate because English is the international language of science, and it offers a rich supply of words to describe and differentiate the finest graduations of meaning.

However, it is easy to lose clarity and meaning in our writing. The prime requirement for scientific English is **short, simple words** and **short, straightforward sentences**.

2. Writing Concisely

> The best English is that which gives the most sense in the fewest short words.
>
> *Journal of Bacteriology* – Instructions to Authors

2.1 Remove Introductory Phrases

- Introductory phrases such as *there is, it is, it will be,* etc. often serve no useful purpose in a sentence. The sentence's meaning will usually be unaltered after dropping such phrases, e.g. "It is the one on the right which is best" becomes "The one on the right is best".
- Occasionally it is more appropriate to shorten, rather than remove introductory phrases such as *it is likely that, probably we can say* by replacing them with *probably* or *perhaps*.
- Retain an introductory phrase if its purpose is to focus the reader's attention (usually used to link paragraphs), e.g. *it is clear that, it is important that.*

2.2   Reword that, which *and* who *clauses*

Omitting words such as *that*, *which* and *who*, along with their associated verbs, will often shorten sentences without affecting their meaning.

For example, "Children look forward to gifts that are given at Christmas" can be rewritten as "Children look forward to gifts at Christmas." The *that* and the associated *are given* are not required and can be removed without altering the meaning of the sentence.

2.3   Eliminate Redundancies

We often use redundancy in spoken language to help clarify our meaning (think of how you speak to a young child). However, in writing, redundancies should be avoided; you must be aware of them and prepared to destroy them.

We commonly use words that are, in effect, useless. For example:

<u>alternative</u> choice	mix <u>together</u>
<u>component</u> part	<u>qualified</u> expert

The underlined words are redundant as they duplicate meaning.

Redundancies can also occur in sentences (and are particularly common in advertising). For example, "This product is completely unique and the very best available". To give a science example, the sentence "In the present paper, the authors show that A affected B at 37°C" does not require the underlined words. They add nothing to the meaning of the sentence.

2.4 Avoid Nominalisation (or camouflaged verbs)

Nouns constructed from verbs are called nominalisation. They are often long words ending in one of the following suffixes: -tion, -ment, -ing, -ance, -ion. Inexperienced writers use nominalisation when they are trying to sound objective, scientific or important. For example, *we made the decisions* **sounds** more impressive than *we decided*, but is dull and ponderous. Changing the nouns into verbs shortens and invigorates the sentences. For example:

> "The *identification* of the pest was carried out by an entomologist ..." becomes "The entomologist *identified* the pest."

> "An *experiment* was carried out to see whether ..." becomes "We *experimented* to see ..."

2.5 Delete Unneeded Prepositions and Prepositional Phrases

Prepositions commonly over-used include *of, in, on, by, to* and *with*. For example "Habits of writing are capable of change" is more simply written as "writing habits can be changed".

Prepositional phrases include *in respect of, for the duration of, in order to*. Their use deadens the writing and makes it boring. For example:

> "During the course of the experiment the group had one problem after another" is more simply written as "Problems arose during the experiment".

3. The Use and Misuse of English

3.1 Errors in Syntax

The word syntax refers to that part of grammar dealing with the way words are put together to form phrases, clauses or sentences. For a sentence to make sense, the words must be presented in a logical sequence. Consider these "bloopers" provided by Day (1992):

"By filtering through Whatman No. 1 filter paper, Smith separated the components."

"A large mass of literature has accumulated on the cell walls of staphylococci."

A golden rule is "if words relate to each other, they should be near each other". For example:

"I visited a farm that was 30 kilometres away on Friday."

The problem with this sentence is that the phrase "on Friday" is too far away from the word it modifies ("visited"), i.e. the syntax is faulty. To make sense, it should be written

"On Friday I visited a farm that was 30 kilometres away."

3.2 Using the Active and Passive 'Voice' of the Verb

Many actions involve two people or things – one that performs the action and one that is affected by the action. The person or thing you want to talk about is usually put first as the subject. So, when you want to talk about something that is the performer of an action, you make it the subject of the verb, and you use an active form of the verb. The other thing is made the object of the verb. For example, *The dog's eaten our dinner* is written in the active voice, because the subject 'dog' is doing the action 'eaten'.

However, you may want to focus on the person or thing affected by an action, which would be the object of an active form of the word. In that instance, you make that person and thing the subject of a passive form of the verb. For example, *Our dinner was eaten by the dog* is written in passive voice, because the subject 'dinner' is not doing the action 'eaten'.

As a general rule, writing in the active voice is more concise, is shorter, and more direct than the passive voice. It is also more personal.

However, it is not compulsory to always use the active voice. If the object of the sentence is more important than the subject, it is appropriate to write in the passive voice.

3.3   *Avoiding Jargon and Verbosity*

Jargon can be defined as "specialised language concerned with a particular subject, culture or profession" (Collins Concise English Dictionary). Of course there will be times when specialised terminology is needed. If such terminology is readily understandable to readers, there is no problem, but if it **may not** be recognisable to some readers, the rule is simple: **avoid jargon**.

Verbosity or pretentiousness afflicts many authors. It is the excessive or even meaningless use of words. Writers with this affliction never **use** anything – they **utilise**. They never **do** – they **perform**. They never **start** – they **initiate**. Other favourites include "at this point in time" (now); "prior to" (before); "subsequent to" (after); "ultimate" (last). **Use simple language**.

Appendix C:
Paragraphing, Punctuation and Pretentiousness: Elements of Style

What is said and the way it is said can be equally important determinants of a successful assignment. This section focuses on three key elements of academic writing – paragraphing, punctuation and appropriate academic style.

1.   Paragraphing

Paragraphing technique can be the factor that distinguishes between a page of muddled ideas and a page of reasoned, logical prose. It is wise to stick to a simple paragraphing style when writing at an undergraduate level, where clarity of thinking and presentation are vitally important. The following principles should guide the way paragraphs are written for undergraduate assignments:

1.1   Every paragraph should contain a single developed idea.

Paragraphs are the building blocks of an assignment. If each paragraph develops one idea fully, the reader will have the opportunity to read and consider one idea at a time. If there is more than one idea in a paragraph, the reader is likely to be confused – or may miss one of the ideas.

1.2   The key idea of the paragraph should be stated in the opening sentence of the paragraph.

This is called using a **deductive** paragraphing style. Because a reader's attention tends to be most focused at the beginning of a chunk of writing, it seems sensible to state a key idea at the beginning of a paragraph. This key idea is called a **topic sentence**. This paragraph and the one preceding it are written in a deductive style.

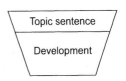

The rest of the sentences can then develop, explain, support the topic sentence. It is a good idea to write the topic sentence in your own words rather than using a quotation.

1.3   A variety of methods can be used to develop topic sentences.

There are many ways to develop an idea. Here are a few of them. Note that each paragraph example is written in a deductive style (i.e. the topic sentence comes **first**).

Develop your topic sentences using:

(i)   **Descriptive or factual details**. This method of paragraph development involves giving a more thorough, concrete explanation of the idea expressed in a general way in the topic sentence. Factual details give measurable, observable or historical information which can be verified. Descriptive details give specific characteristics of the subject being discussed.

        e.g.   Planning is a vital aspect of every organisation. It gives a company direction and a sense of purpose. It draws all members of the organisation together and makes every decision clearer. Without planning an organisation may founder either through lack of direction or through divisive directions.

(ii)   **Illustrations and examples**. The writer may use several brief examples or one extended illustration. The illustration may be factual or hypothetical (i.e. invented for the purpose of illustration).

        e.g.   Planning is a vital aspect of every organisation. For Southern Motors, a designer of small engines in New Zealand, it was a life saver. The company was foundering for lack of direction, trying to fill needs in conflicting markets. When the new general manager, Colin Appleyard, was appointed, his first step was to draw all the operational managers together to construct strategic and tactical plans. The decision was made to halve the number of products and to target specific markets. Now, three years later, the company is going from strength to strength.

(iii)   **Definitions**. These can be used to explain concepts or terms which may be unfamiliar to the reader. It is generally more effective to attempt your own definition than to copy from a dictionary. A definition is often more effective when combined with an illustration or example.

e.g.   Planning is vital to all organisations. Planning is a broad term. It involves many processes – forming a mission statement, designing a strategic plan, defining goals and establishing operational methods. It has implications for every level of the organisation.

(iv)   **Authority**. Finally, it is common to use authority to develop the topic sentence. This is appropriate and useful because it positions your work within an academic debate – it shows that your idea is supported by people who may have more credibility and standing than you do.

e.g.   Planning is vital to all organisations. Sanders (1993) sees it as "the skeleton of the organisation, determining the structure and capabilities of a company" (p. 16). Other researchers (Carlton 1994; Fiach & Paine 1995) emphasise its capacity to create a sense of direction and unity.

1.4   Finally, use connectives between and within paragraphs to unify your writing.

Words which signal logical relationships between ideas also help to clarify the message for the reader. In analytical writing, each sentence and paragraph should be related logically to the sentence or paragraph which precedes or follows it. This connection is often implicit in the writing. Good writers also have an extensive vocabulary of connectives which signal explicitly the relationships between sentences and paragraphs. These connectives clarify the line of thought being developed. Six types of logical relationships are set out in the following list.

Logical Connective	Examples
Signals for Addition	also, besides, in addition, likewise, moreover, similarly, furthermore
Signals for Reversal	despite this, instead, nonetheless, nevertheless, on the other hand, still, however, alternatively
Signals for a Chain of Reasoning	therefore, as a result, accordingly, because of this, hence, consequently, thus
Signals for Specific Illustration	for example, for instance, specifically, to illustrate
Signals for Specifying an Idea	that is, namely, in short
Signals for a Time Relationship	then, afterwards, soon, eventually, later, meanwhile, as, thereafter, sometime, presently

2.   Punctuation

2.1   The Full Stop or Period

This is used to mark the end of a sentence. It may be replaced by the question mark(?) or (rarely) the exclamation mark(!).

- Have you ever wondered why leaves fall off trees in the autumn?
- It is very important to use punctuation correctly! Think of what would happen if you didn't! Readers might be misled! Don't risk it! Attend a lecture on punctuation today!

2.2   The Comma

This is used to mark off bits of a longer sentence to make meaning clearer.

1. Joining two sentences with a conjunction:

    - I came out to Massey, and I went to my lecture.
    - I tried to get some milk, but the dairy had sold out.

2. Where you have added bits to the basic sentence:

    (a)   as openers:
    - However, I got some at the supermarket.
    - In the end, I borrowed some from my flatmate.
    (b)   in the middle, usually between the subject and verb:
    - The baby, who had cried all night, went to sleep at dawn.
    - My only transport, a brand new mountain bike, was stolen yesterday.
    (c)   as enders:
    - The baby went to sleep at dawn, to his parents' relief.
    - I borrowed some socks from my flatmate, that generous soul.

3. To list items in a series:

    - I am studying German, English, philosophy and history.
    - Whether you are singing, playing an instrument, or dancing, expressing yourself with music is relaxing and energising.

4. Writing addresses or large numbers, or any other potentially confusing situation:

- 235B Ponsonby Road North, Auckland (could be Ponsonby Road, North Auckland).
- NZ$3,000,000.

2.3   The Semicolon

This has two common uses.

1. Joining two complete sentences which are closely related, or which reflect each other:

   - We all enjoy our flat; it has a great atmosphere.
   - There are the benefits of sharing; there are also the disadvantages of lack of privacy.

2. Listing complex items which need commas in themselves:

   - When leaving New Zealand you should have a current passport, issued by your own government; a re-entry permit, which you can apply for at the Immigration Department; travellers cheques, obtainable at your bank; and a good book, which you can buy at the airport before you leave.

2.4   The Colon

This is a clue that something is coming, a sort of introductory flourish. You will probably use it in two situations.

1. To introduce a quote of more than one sentence:

   - Wolf (1993, p. 190) sees this situation as complex:

     We are all struggling against impulses that draw us backwards, and compensate psychologically for the strangeness of a great leap forward. The backlash wasn't generated just by men; part of the stasis women experience derives from their own ambivalence about entering the alien land of equality.

2. To introduce a smaller quote if it says what you have just said in different words:

- The situation is no better in England, according to Wolf: "The same absence of women on political discussion programmes in Britain was noted by the *Independent*" (Wolf 1993, p. 89).

3. To introduce a list:

- You need only a few basic ingredients to make scones: flour, baking powder, butter and milk.

2.5   The Apostrophe

This seems to be the most difficult punctuation mark to use correctly, but there are really only two main uses for it.

1. To indicate letters have been left out of a word:
> won't (will not)
> I'll (I will)
> shan't (shall not)
> we'll (we shall or we will)
> I'd (I would or I had)
> you'd (you had)
> it's (it is – compared to its in (iii) below)

2. To indicate possession:

    (a)   for **singular nouns**, add 's:

the man's name	the child's toy
the student's room	a cat's dinner
Mary's film	a girl's birthday
James's novels	

    (b)   for **plural nouns formed by adding s**, just add ':

the students' flat	all girls' uniforms
four cats' dinners	both Marys' mothers

    (c)   for **plural nouns formed in other ways**, add 's:

men's names   children's toys
women's clothing

(d)   for words that already have lots of s sounds,
         just add ':

         Rameses' monument   Jesus' words
         scissors' blade

There is **no need for an apostrophe** in these situations:

(i)   reference to decades, as in the 1860s, or the 1920s.

(ii)   when making a plural of a word ending in a vowel.

         Tomatoes, potatoes and bananas are perfectly all right, but some
         greengrocers seem driven to write tomato's, potato's and banana's.

(iii)   the possessive of a pronoun, as in ours, yours, hers and its
         (meaning 'belonging to it' – compare with it's in 1. above).

NB:	it's	means	it is	–	letter left out
	its	means	belonging to it	–	no apostrophe

2.6   The Dash

This is used like a comma, but gives greater emphasis. It may be used singly or in a
pair. Try to avoid using this too often; it gives your prose a choppy feel.

* We all got there eventually – and then it was time to leave.
* We take turns – at least we try to – at shopping and cooking.

2.7   The Bracket

Again, this is used to mark off a thought which is relevant but not crucial to the
sentence. It is less emphatic (smoother) than the dash.

* My mother worked for a legal firm (which has since been sold) on the corner of
  Featherston Street.
* The landlord is always coming around (to check up, we suspect), so we are

looking for another flat.

Note the comma which is needed between "around" and "so" (see the first rule of commas, above) is **after** the bracket. **Never** put a comma before a bracket!

2.8 *The Ellipse*

This indicates that something has been left out of a quote, or, occasionally, it is put in for effect at the end of a sentence – usually an indication that the writer has 'left something out' for you to fill in for yourself.

- "Management ... is a major component ..." (Rice 1991, p. 17).
- Then, just as John saw the lights of his house clearly, a large shadow moved between him and his goal, and he felt a damp, clammy arm pull him inexorably towards a reeking, drooling mouth ...

The small-arms retailer meets the small arms retailer.

2.9 The Hyphen

This small punctuation mark can be very useful to tie together two words and avoid confusion.

- A Dutch-cheese importer is anyone who imports Dutch cheese; a Dutch cheese importer is a Dutch person who imports any sort of cheese.
- A small-arms retailer will sell you a handgun; a small arms retailer is a short person who sells a wide range of guns.

3.   Style

Finally, a few words about the style of academic writing. Style is a difficult issue to define and explain. You should remember that, even in academic writing, your main concern should be to communicate your ideas clearly to a reader. Style, then, should be designed on the basis of three things:

- The nature of your message.
- The purpose of the sender.
- The needs of the reader.

Most academic writing at an undergraduate level (essays in particular) should be aimed at an audience which is intelligent but not well-informed on your subject.
In particular, you should follow these guidelines:

- Sentences should be short, and they should contain a single idea.
- Write in the active voice.
- Cut out unnecessary words.
- Do not use personal pronouns (I, we, you) unless you are told you can.
- If you have a choice between a long word and a short word, choose the short word.
- If you need to use jargon, define your terms.
- Use gender neutral and culturally safe language.
- Be direct.
- Aim for clarity.

The last point is perhaps the most important point, and incorporates many of the other items on the list. Do not make the mistake of thinking that complex sentences, a pretentious, convoluted style and long Latinate words will impress your reader. Such a style is more likely to obscure your ideas. Write in a simple, clear yet formal manner, using language which you fully understand, and you will communicate with your reader.

Appendix D:
Using Inclusive Language

In accordance with their EEO policies, most universities and polytechnics are now committed to promoting equity through the use of language which is inclusive of all groups in society.

We use language to describe the world and ourselves and others in relation to each other and the world. We use language to express our thoughts and attitudes, but also to acquire those thoughts and attitudes. Language changes, and with it the meaning of words. For example, 'to be gay' has a very different meaning in the early 21st century than it did in the 1930s.

There are two aims to this section: the first is to explain the reasons why we all need to use inclusive language in our communication, and the second is to provide guidelines to help you use language which allows all people to be treated equally, with courtesy and respect.

1.   Why Use Inclusive Language?

There are a number of reasons for using inclusive language. The most persuasive is that if we want to reach all people with our message, then we should not treat some people as if they are invisible.

A snapshot of a typical organisation or working community 50 years ago would reflect an almost exclusively white work force. These days, while there may still be a predominance of white male faces, the snapshot is far more likely to present a more balanced gender picture, as well as include Maori, Asian, Pacific Island and other ethnic representation. Statistics give us a picture of New Zealand as a country populated by people from many nations, and our organisations increasingly reflect this multi-ethnic face. More and more women are entering or returning to paid employment outside the home.

It is important that our language reflects the society in which we live. The person who writes "every nursery manager should ensure he follows his business plan" is assuming that all nursery managers are male (which is certainly not the case) or that those nursery managers who are not male do not mind being thought of as male – which is definitely not a reasonable assumption! Similarly, any expression that implies that women are less than men, or that people with disabilities are incapable of making a useful contribution, or that people of a certain ethnic group are different and therefore less worthy, is discriminatory. Human Rights legislation is now in place to ensure that people are not discriminated against in the workplace, or, for that matter, in the community as a whole.

Historically, the English language has had a tendency to exclude women by the use of terms such as manpower, manning the desk, or businessman when there are perfectly adequate terms which can be used and which include women. Clichés and generalisations have also served to overlook the contribution of women: expressions such as 'founding fathers' imply women made no contribution, when in fact they worked every bit as hard at different but complementary tasks. Some people will think these points are trivial, but the issue is important to those who do feel excluded.

2. Guidelines

- Avoid stereotypes.
- Use language appropriately.
- Rephrase where necessary to avoid offence or exclusion.

The word man is used to refer both to an adult male and to people as a species. When the reference is intended to include both men and women, there are several alternatives.

For example

manpower	labour, work force
manning the desk	staffing the desk
mankind	humanity, people, human beings
the average man	the average person

Rather than use the generic **he** to denote third person singular, you can rephrase the sentence, or accept **their** as a singular pronoun.

For example

when a student enrols, he must	when students enrol, they must
when a researcher presents his findings	when a researcher presents their findings
each worker must service his machine	workers must service their machines

Do not assume that people who work in certain occupations are of a particular gender.

For example

farmers and their wives	farmers and their partners
woman doctor, male nurse	doctor, nurse
businessman	executive, businessperson

Girl should only be used to describe someone still at school. Use woman or young woman. A female shop assistant should not be called a salesgirl as a male is not usually called a salesboy.

Most people with a disability are healthy and need not be described as "suffering from", "afflicted with" or "a victim of". There is a difference between being hearing impaired and profoundly deaf, and not all people who are sight impaired are blind.

For example

Chris suffers from epilepsy	Chris has epilepsy
Kim is confined to a wheelchair	Kim uses a wheelchair

Appendix E:
Exam Skills

1. Identifying Probable Exam Topics

Reading notes, textbooks and study guides over and over again is not the best way to prepare for exam essays. It is important to try to identify and prepare topics, key themes and/or issues which will probably be set. To do this:

- *Read through the notes you have made*
  The purposes of this are to refresh your memory about the content of the paper and to give you a fair indication of the probable scope of the exam paper. This should also remind you of the key concepts and issues which have been covered during the year, the main divisions into which the materials covered fit, and the rationale underlying the whole paper. Note, in particular, the extent to which certain topics and sections have been covered – this is usually a good indication of their importance and the likelihood of their turning up in the exam. Note also the emphasis placed on these topics/sections by your lecturers (or in your study guides).

- *Look at past exam papers*
  You do this to identify the topics/themes/issues which are usually covered and to become familiar with the format of the exam. Make sure, however, that you are aware of any changes to lecturers, paper content, and/or exam format that may have occurred since these previous exam papers were set.

Of course, you can never really be certain that a particular topic will turn up, and it is very difficult to predict the precise wording and focus of the questions in the exam. Therefore:

- *Always prepare more topics than will be required in the exam*
  For example, if you have to write four essays in the exam, prepare at least six topics. Also make sure that you are at least reasonably familiar with the other topics, themes and issues covered in the paper even if you do not prepare for them thoroughly – just in case.

- *Prepare essay topics comprehensively*
  What this means is that you should prepare to the extent that you are more or less certain you will be able to answer any question on the topic irrespective of wording or focus.

2.   Preparation and Revision Activities

- *As noted earlier, prepare likely topics, key themes and/or issues*

- *Collect and summarise all relevant information on the topic*
  This includes definitions, factual statements, evidence, examples, opinions, descriptions, and other similar information. This can be collected mainly from your notes, but also (if necessary) from study guides, texts, assigned readings, handouts, and other relevant sources.

- *Organise the information*
  Organise these under theme headings such as: definitions/descriptions, supporting evidence, strengths/weaknesses, applications/limitations, similarities/differences, and so on.

- *Make written summaries and/or construct 'mind maps' of the points and information you have gathered and organised*

- *Check the material you have revised against past exam papers*
  In doing this, examine which questions relate to the material you have been revising. Try to get a clear understanding of what points you would need to cover in order to answer each relevant question.

- *Try framing your own exam questions*
  As you learn and better understand the materials you are revising, you will probably start getting some ideas about questions that are likely to be asked for each topic. See if you can quickly jot down important points and other information that you would include in your answers should these questions be asked.

- *Write trial answers to some questions*
  Especially if you have time, it may be very useful to try writing answers to some questions (e.g. ones you have thought up, or ones from previous exam papers) without looking at your notes and within the time limit of the exam. If you are short of time, just write these trial answers in note form – paying

attention particularly to the relevant and important points you would include (and can/cannot remember) and the way you would structure your answers. Some lecturers and tutors may be willing to skim through these trial efforts and comment on your performance. Comments from other students may also be helpful. But the greatest value of writing trial answers comes from getting practice in working under exam conditions (namely: thinking, remembering, writing, structuring, etc.). It will also indicate how much you can write on a question within a given time limit.

- *For an open book exam, organise your materials well beforehand*
  This is important so that you can use them quickly and efficiently within the time constraints of the exam. So make sure your notes will be easy to use, and that you will be able to find relevant things quickly in your texts (use markers).

3.　What to Aim for in Essay Exams

- Clarity of focus on the set topic (i.e. answer the question given).
- Comprehensive coverage of the central issues directly relating to the topic (as is possible within the limits of the exam time).
- To be able to show that you have systematically revised the relevant course materials, and have understood them well.
- A reasonably well-structured and logical argument (within the constraints of the exam condition – e.g. there is little or no time for redrafting).
- To be able to make clear, relevant and important points that will gain you marks.
- Clarity and conciseness in expression of ideas, concepts and arguments.
- Legible handwriting.

4.　Taking Essay-type Exams

Essay-type exams, just like other types of exams, demand a quick response. It is also important that exam answers are accurately directed to the terms of the set questions. The following points and strategies are important.

- *If there are alternatives, be decisive in selecting the question(s) you will answer*
  It is a waste of valuable time to oscillate from one question to another, or to write plans for all alternative questions first before deciding which one you will answer. The time you waste on indecisiveness can be more effectively used in producing well thought out and well-structured answers.

- *Make sure you understand the questions you will answer*
Look closely at the wording of each question and make sure you have understood the content you must cover and the way you are directed to answer.

- *Plan each of your answers first (on the exam paper itself) before you start writing*
Jot down points, facts, names, dates and other relevant information, then quickly organise and structure these. Planning is quite important in essay type exams because you can only write one draft. This means that before starting to write you need to be reasonably clear on the points you will make, the direction of your argument, and so on. (Note, however, that planning needs to be done quickly – not in a take-all-the-time-in-the-world fashion.)

- *For the structure of the essay, follow the structure of the question*
So, for example, if the question asks you to "Discuss ... then evaluate ...", make sure that the first section of your essay focuses on a discussion of the relevant points and issues, and the second section deals with the evaluation (of whatever the question asks you to evaluate).

- *Leave at least a half of a page at the end of each essay you write*
This is in case you remember something else later that you would want to add to your answer.

- *Try to leave yourself a little time at the end to quickly re-read and check the answers you have written*
Check your essay for clarity, correctness and accuracy of facts (make sure you have written what you really intended to write!), and legibility.

Appendix F:
Student Model of a Report to a Client

Report to the Minister of Science and Technology on the Major Threats and Current Protection of the Siberian Tiger

(4.10.04)

By: K. Tootell
To: Hon. Mr Carter

ScienceWords
PO BOX 498
Palmerston North

4 October 2004

Hon. Murray Carter
Minister of Science and Technology
PO Box 787
Wellington

Dear Mr Carter

Please find enclosed the report requested by Angela Farmer on 24 July 2004. The report focuses on the threats to, and the current protection of the Siberian tiger. The key findings include:

1. The major threats to the Siberian tiger are declination of its habitat and prey, canine distemper disease, and poaching.
2. There are several protection plans that aim to conserve the Siberian tiger population in the wild.
3. The New Zealand and Australian governments – or charitable trusts within these counties – should consider how they can contribute to this international preservation programme.

Feel free to contact me at the above address if further information is required.

Yours sincerely

Kim Tootell
ScienceWords Consultant

Table of Contents

1.0 Introduction

Siberian tigers are the largest of all tiger species, living mainly in coniferous forests of Far East Russia. They are generally solitary animals, living in a vast territory. 360–406 remain in the wild, classing them as an endangered species (World Wildlife Fund, 2004). Tigers need to be protected in order for them to survive. They are threatened in several ways.

The objective of this report is to investigate major threats and provide information about the current conservation plans to protect this species, so the New Zealand and Australian governments can consider whether to be involved in the funding of preservation campaigns. Key findings include: a reduction in habitat, the diminishing number of prey, canine distemper disease and poaching are the major threats. Current projects designed to conserve these tigers must be continued if the Siberian tiger population is to survive. Australia and New Zealand do have a part to play in these projects and should consider becoming involved.

This report refers only to the main threats, and protection plans proposed by prominent organisations devoted to conserving wildlife.

Limitations of this report include the restrictions on word length, access to academic journals and availability of up-to-date information.

2.0 Discussion

2.1 The Siberian tigers' habitat and population has decreased by 95% in the past 100 years. This is due to disturbances, including human population growth, logging of forests, forest fires, dam building, mining and road construction (WWF, 2002, 2004; Ipzoo, 2004). Female tigers' territory is approximately 450km^2. The Sikhot-Alin-Zapovendik Reserve, in the Amur River drainage in Russia is 4000km^2. This gives space for only 10 tigresses (Wildlife Conservation Society, 2003–2004). National parks and reserves create a hospitable environment for tigers, however the WCS and WWF are working to extend the conservation beyond these specific sites to vast landscapes (WWF, 2002). Corridors between the conservation sites will increase protection of the tigers (WWF, 2004).

2.2   It is vital that the population of Siberian tiger's prey is sustained because without food the tigers will not survive. Only 5–10% of their hunting attempts are successful (WWF, 2004; Sinor, S. 2001). 85% of their diet consists of wild boar and red deer (appendix A). Human disturbance and heavy snowfall destroys their habitat (WCS, 2003–2004; Ipzoo, 2004; Cutlip, 2002). An imbalance in the food chain will not be beneficial to the ecosystem as a whole. The American Forests group has provided grants for tree planting (appendix A).

2.3   Canine distemper is a disease that is fatal to cats. Dr. Quigley and a team of wildlife vets are working to address the problem. Quigley says "With less than 500 tigers in the wild in Russia, this could be a very serious threat that could contribute to the loss of a severely endangered population." (Delaney & Saunter, 2004, para. 3). It can be contracted from domestic animals and circulate quickly through the tiger population. "67% of all dogs sampled have been exposed to the virus." (Delaney & Saunter, 2004, para. 5). Quigley believes that as people and their domestic animals continue to encroach upon tiger habitat, the disease becomes an ever-increasing threat to tiger conservation worldwide (Delaney & Saunter, 2004, para 7). Her team is training Russian vets in wildlife health and teaching them about disease transmission and handling of tigers in tiger-human conflict situations. (Delaney, & Saunter, 2004)

2.4   Tigers have been killed for many years. In the 20th Century in Russia they were considered pests, because they preyed on livestock (Nowell & Jackson, 1998). Tigers have been shot, hunted, snared, poisoned and electrocuted. (WWF, 2004)

Hunting was banned in the 1947 (Gangloff et al., 2000), however Gorbachev's reform in the Soviet Government led to illegal poaching as there was an increase in trade activity across Russia's borders (Lee, 1997). Some Asian countries demand tiger bones, skin, and organs on the black market. Tiger parts are worth "US$5000–$10,000 on the black market." (Goodrich, 2004, p6). The Convention on International Trade in Endangered Species of Wild Fauna and Flora (CITES) treaty was signed in 1994 to declare tiger trade illegal. However, reports show only six of the fourteen tiger-range countries are committed to the treaty (Lee, 1997). Russia has a domestic law protecting tigers, yet is not a member of CITES.

Research has been undertaken into the medicinal uses of tiger parts. WWF has been working with traditional medicine communities in CITES countries to eliminate the use of tiger parts (WWF, 2002). The World Conservation Union has cooperated with these groups to identify key trade routes (WWF, 2004). Tiger bones are believed to "cure joint and back pains, paralysis, and muscle spasms; its brain is used to cure acne." (Lee, 1997, Description section, para. 2). The use of the tiger for healing is rooted deep in some Asian cultures. They believe the tiger gives them strength and virility (Lee, 1997).

2.5   A series of protection plans have been proposed to conserve the Siberian tiger. Projects under TRAFFIC (the largest wildlife trade monitoring network) include Project 12: "Understanding the Market for Tiger Bone Medicines". This aims to evaluate the effectiveness of bans on trading tiger bone in major overseas Asian communities and make recommendations to control illegal trade. Surveys of medicines, pharmacies, and the current bans. Other projects include Project 44: "Protection of the Amur Tiger and its Habitat in the Russian Far East". The activities include:

1. Supporting anti-poaching operations by patrolling outside protected areas.

2. Improving trade-ban enforcements by assisting the Russian customs with technical training,

3. Conserving tiger habitats by increasing ranger forces in reserves, establishing new reserves, and protecting corridors between these areas.

4. Increasing public awareness through education.

5. Monitoring the impact of timber and mining on tiger populations, and promoting sustainable forestry practices. (Nowell & Jackson, 1998)

The Siberian Tiger Project (1992) has led onto the current 'Siberian Tiger Conservation Plan'. This was formed by the WCS in 2002. (WCS, 2003–2004). They attached radio collars to 36 tigers and monitored their activity. These are used today, giving information about "… tiger social structure, land use patterns, feeding habits, reproduction, mortality, and tigers' relation to other inhabitants of the ecosystem." (WCS, 2003–2004, Siberian tiger Project, para. 1). Valuable knowledge gained includes 80% of tiger mortality is due to humans. 2.4 cubs are born per adult female every 21 months, yet 50% of cubs die before they are 1year old (WCS, 2003–2004). By 2010 they hope to have 100 female tigers in each landscape. The plan involves having focal landscape coordinators who act on the ground to eliminate poaching, monitor and evaluate individual and overall progress of projects, supervise, oversee and communicate with wider networks of conservationists. Teams monitor the tigers, by trapping and anaesthetising them, checking temperature, teeth, gums, coat, weight, breathing, and collecting blood, tissue and hair samples for genetic analysis (Goodrich, 2004). Reports from this analysis provide invaluable data.

3.0 Conclusions

3.1 A major threat to the Siberian tiger population is the reduction of its habitat caused by human disturbance.

3.2 Another threat is the declining number of the tigers' prey.

3.3 Canine distemper poses a dangerous threat to the tiger population.

3.4 Poaching for the illegal trade of tiger parts for medicinal purposes poses a great risk to the Siberian tiger.

3.5 There are plans in place that aim to protect this endangered species.

3.6 New Zealand and Australia are, at present, not involved in conservation efforts.

4.0 Recommendations

4.1 A broad approach should be taken to sustain the ecosystem needs of humans and tigers in the designated areas. Roads must be closed at night, if not in use. Restrictions should be applied to the construction of new roads. Speed limits must be enforced. Human activity in tiger populated areas should be controlled.

4.2 Efforts should be made to conserve the tigers' prey – wild boar and deer.

4.3 A vaccine should be developed for canine distemper. This should be accompanied by a campaign to educate the public to reduce likelihood of infection of domestic animals. If New Zealand and Australia are serious about contributing to international preservation programmes, this might be an area where the Australian and New Zealand Governments could consider providing funding.

4.4 It is important that authorities enforce laws, monitor and patrol areas inside and outside national parks and reserves and close roads to reduce poaching. Further research is needed into the use of tigers for medicinal purposes. Again, this is an area where government could consider contributing either money or expertise.

4.5 Government and community support of proposed conservation plans will ensure they are implemented. Economic incentives may be necessary to gain this support. It is possible for our government, or charitable trusts within our countries, to raise funding for these plans.

5.0 Reference List

6.0 Bibliography

7.0 Appendix A